For

Best wishes

Happy 2015

[signature]

January, 2015

IDITAROD
ADVENTURES

Iditarod Adventures

TALES FROM MUSHERS ALONG THE TRAIL

By LEW FREEDMAN

Illustrations by JON VAN ZYLE

ALASKA
NORTHWEST
BOOKS®

Library of Congress Cataloging-in-Publication Data
Freedman, Lew.
  Iditarod adventures : tales from mushers along the trail / by Lew Freedman ;
illustrations by Jon Van Zyle.
     pages cm
  Includes index.
  ISBN 978-1-941821-28-2 (pbk.)
  ISBN 978-1-941821-53-4 (hardbound)
  ISBN 978-1-941821-52-7 (e-book)
  1. Iditarod (Race) 2. Sled dog racing—Alaska. 3. Mushers—Alaska—Biography. 4.
Women mushers—Alaska—Biography. I. Van Zyle, Jon II. Title.
  SF440.15.F735 2015
  798.8'309798—dc23
                          2014025964

Map: Gray Mouse Graphics
Designer: Rudy Ramos

Published by Alaska Northwest Books®
An imprint of

GRAPHIC ARTS
BOOKS®

P.O. Box 56118
Portland, Oregon 97238-6118
503-254-5591
www.graphicartsbooks.com

Contents

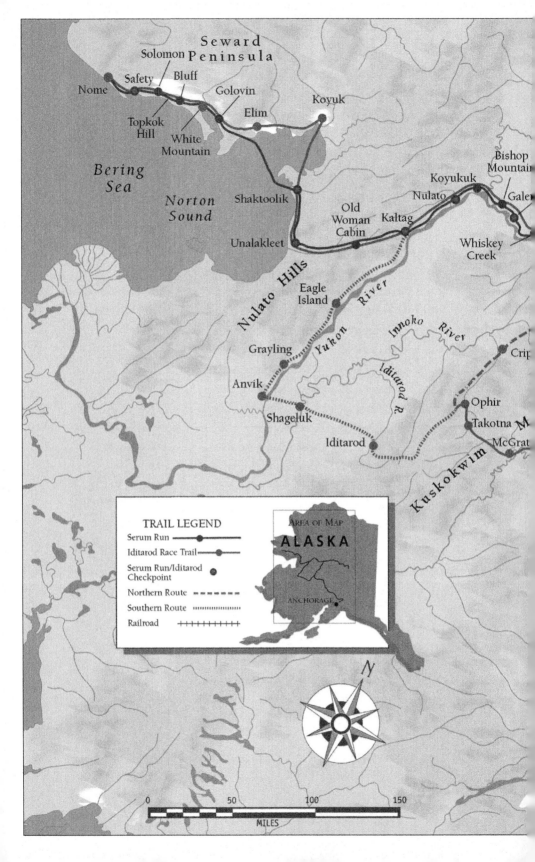

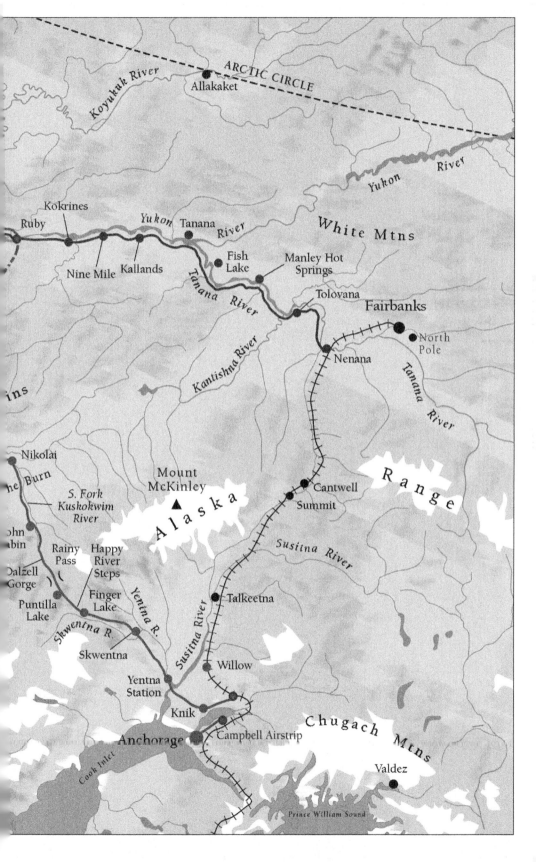

INTRODUCTION

Probably the coldest I've ever been taking notes was standing at the finish line of the Iditarod Trail Sled Dog Race in Nome in 1991 as the clock inched toward 2 A.M. amidst the reports of winner Rick Swenson approaching on Front Street.

The temperature was minus-twenty-five degrees and the windchill made it feel like fifty below. I stood in place, surrounded by the crowd of spectators, for more than an hour. When Swenson crossed the finish line for his record fifth victory—a mark that still stands—my fingers felt as wooden as the pencil they tried to grasp.

Those of us who waited for the arrival of the king were likely equally frozen, despite the warmest of wardrobes hugging our bodies. It was just a fact of life that if you were associating with the 1,049-mile race between Anchorage and Nome on the Bering Sea Coast, that at one time or another during the event that lasted about ten days, you were going to be shivering.

Even if the wind whipped through those of us hanging out at the finish line near the burled arch that marked the end of the trail, we had it easy. It was always colder, snowier, windier, harder going out there for the mushers and their dogs, in the vast expanse of Alaska, the Last Frontier. No one had any illusions about that.

Termed "The Last Great Race on Earth," the Iditarod, named for an old gold mining town in the state's Interior, represented the ultimate wilderness challenge. It was man (or woman) against the elements, with only sled dogs for companions, comfort, and transportation. The Iditarod is a throwback race, an event with its origins stemming from a bygone era.

No matter who you are, a nervous novice testing himself on the trail for the first time, or a hardened veteran, each year, each March, when the race leaves the big city of Anchorage, the weather and the trail can play havoc with wise plans, and grand hopes. No one knows whether a sled will encounter ice or snow drifts. No one knows whether a musher will contend with frigid temperatures or warm ones. Will it be sunny? Will it be gloomy? Each musher takes his chances and hopes he is prepared for anything.

Since its founding in 1973, mainly through the efforts of the late Joe Redington Sr. and a team of helpers he organized, the Iditarod has implanted itself in Alaskans' minds as the most unifying and popular event that the union's largest state at 586,000 square miles can wrap its arms around.

While ostensibly a sporting event—the one Alaska is most proud of— the Iditarod is more than that. It represents a way of life. It is an event that is very much of a place, its size and scope giving heft to the boast that it is the grandest sled-dog race in the world. Redington's dual dream of ensuring that the husky dog species was perpetuated and the Iditarod Trail preserved has long been achieved.

Beyond that the Iditarod has become a symbol of Alaska, much like Mount McKinley, the 20,320-foot-high mountain that is the tallest in North America, as its reputation has spread and spread, the one recurring event that nearly everyone identifies with the forty-ninth state.

The race has spawned legends and lore, heroes and icons. Rick Swenson of Two Rivers is the only musher with five victories. The late Susan Butcher won the race four times. As has Martin Buser of Big Lake, Jeff King of Denali Park, Doug Swingley of Lincoln, Montana, and Lance Mackey of Fairbanks.

Family dynasties have evolved. Dick Mackey helped Redington stage the first Iditarod and then outraced Swenson by one second in 1978 in the closest race of them all. His son Rick won in 1983 and another son Lance won those four times. Jason, a third son, is still racing. Dan Seavey recorded a top finish in the first Iditarod. His son Mitch has won twice and Dan's grandson Dallas won in 2012 and 2014.

Mushers have been separated from their dog teams in forbidding weather and had to walk miles to safety, not to be confused with the last checkpoint of Safety, twenty-two miles from Nome. They have somehow navigated blown-in trails where visibility was practically nil. They have suffered frostbite. For one reason or another, even simply dog-tired fatigue, it is always a battle to reach Nome. There a good night's rest, a hot meal, and warmth dispensed by loved ones are on the agenda to soothe the aching body. There is also the glow of satisfaction in the form of prize money if one does well, or the simpler prize of an Iditarod belt buckle awarded for reaching the terminus of the trail.

Not everyone can be a champion. The Iditarod appeals to Everyman and Everywoman, those motivated by the spirit of adventure, the challenge of competition, or the love of the land. Some mushers, Martin Buser, Jeff King, DeeDee Jonrowe, Sonny Lindner, and others, have made virtual careers out of competing in the thousand-mile race each year, raising dogs in their kennels, mushing dogs, suborning other goals, to the Iditarod. Some are full-time, professional mushers, living off sponsorships, appearances, and prize money. Some are hooked by the race and have no desire to remove the hook.

It is often said that the Iditarod is to Alaska what the Kentucky Derby is to Louisville or the Indianapolis 500 is to Indiana. Each year there is great anticipation as the first Saturday in March draws near. Fans have their favorites, for many different reasons. They admire excellence among the front-running contenders. They wish to see a Native musher take a turn, or a woman cross the finish line first. As the mushers work their way across the state, passing through the small villages of almost unoccupied locales that make up the checkpoints, in Rohn and Nikolai, McGrath and Unalakleet, Anvik and Grayling, their presence is eagerly anticipated.

Iditarod mushers are so well-known that many of them are referred to by fans by first names only, as if they are friends and neighbors more than the best athletes in their sport. In a way they are friends and neighbors the rest of the year when they are not busy on the trail.

Whether a musher has completed the Iditarod once, or two dozen times, chances are he or she will have a story to tell. In *Iditarod Adventures*, mushers explain why they have chosen this rugged lifestyle, what has kept them in long-distance mushing, and what types of experiences they have endured along that unforgiving trail between Anchorage and Nome during their careers.

There are twenty-eight individuals included whose stories are related, and not every one of those people spend their Iditarod time on the trail. Included also are administrators who organize the event and make sure it happens every year, volunteers, and others whose connection to the Iditarod is self-evident even if they don't have an official title.

One thing all of these Iditarod people agree upon is that none of them have seen it all. Each time the Iditarod unfolds it is a new and fresh adventure. Each time a musher steps upon the sled runners and urges the team onward from the starting line, he is plunging into the unknown.

Never was this more evident than in the 2014 race. The trail over the first two hundred miles was brutal, devoid of snow and filled with large boulders. Sleds and human bones were broken and in one day alone twelve mushers scratched. Then the trail became swift and smooth and mushers were on a record pace to finish. Abruptly, on the Bering Sea Coast, the weather changed, the wind blowing violently up to sixty-five miles per hour. Just when it seemed certain that the top three had been sorted out, the Iditarod fooled everyone again, shaking up the final standings.

The reminder was very vivid: A new script is written each March and no one knows the ending in advance.

—Lew Freedman
March 2014

The 100th All Alaska Sweepstakes commemorative poster.

CHAPTER 1

Martin BUSER

orn in Zurich, Switzerland, in 1958, Martin Buser is one of the most decorated of Iditarod champions. A four-time winner of the race, Buser, who lives in Big Lake, Alaska, made his debut in the Iditarod in 1980 after moving to the United States the year before. Buser's early dog training came through working as a handler for famed Alaska sprint musher Earl Norris in Willow.

During his lengthy career Buser has set speed records along the trail and was even sworn in as an American citizen under the burled arch on Front Street in Nome. He and his wife, Kathy Chapoton, a retired teacher, named their sons *Nikolai* and *Rohn* after checkpoints along the Iditarod Trail.

The 2014 Iditarod—in which he set the early pace—was Buser's thirty-first race. He captured the crown in 1992, 1994, 1997, and 2002. His time of eight days, twenty-two hours, forty-six minutes, two seconds in 2002 was a milestone as the first Iditarod completed in under nine days. Among Buser's many Iditarod honors are being a four-time recipient of the race Humanitarian Award, a two-time winner of the Sportsmanship Award, and being chosen as the most inspirational musher in 2005.

In addition to his four triumphs, eight other times Buser has finished in the top five of the Iditarod standings. A genial musher, Buser has reveled in visiting the small villages along the trail and has been one of the most popular mushers in the race.

Buser is one of a small number of dog mushers who have been able to become true professionals, whose entire lifestyle, raising dogs and racing dogs, providing lectures and demonstrations to the public, has enabled him to make a living from the sport.

My first Iditarod was in 1980 and I was twenty-two years old. My first language was Swiss-German so I was learning a lot of things. I drove Siberian huskies. It was a fluke that I lucked into them. I was working for Earl and Natalie Norris and they sent me out on the trail. After the first one they sent me out on the trail again the next year so they must have seen something in me, my interaction with the dogs, or something. So my first Iditarods in 1980 and 1981 I ran with Siberian huskies and I got hooked on running the Iditarod, hooked on the sport, the lifestyle and the complexity of the race.

When I first came to Alaska I had a one-year window in mind. I simply wanted to be away from home for a year, kind of a year abroad, with no intention to immigrate, no intention to make mushing a full-time vocation. I just basically wanted to get into the workforce for a year. I had all kinds of job offers at home after finishing my schooling. Of course, in Europe you are looked at as a fool if you don't take a job offer and I had six or seven possibilities.

My field was horticulture. I figured that if I had that many opportunities at home I could go abroad for a year and still have one of those opportunities open. I had finished second in my class. I joke that the guy that was first in the class was a nerd, so he didn't have nearly as much fun as me.

So I had no intention of not returning to Switzerland and working for a living and being a typical central European who was married to his job and maybe secondarily to his spouse, you know, in that order of importance. But then things started to go to the dogs and after two Iditarods I knew Alaska was for me. I knew I wanted to stay in Alaska and in the meantime I had a couple of epiphanies, about how the Iditarod could be done differently and how the dogs could be trained.

But I had nothing. I had literally come to the United States with a backpack and a couple of pairs of blue jeans. Clearly, I had no means of supporting—barely supporting—myself, let alone a dog team. So after I finished handling for Earl and Natalie Norris, I had to go to work and I first worked as a youth counselor. I worked with emotionally disturbed kids. That's when I met Kathy. I joke that I was one of her clients at Alaska Children's Services in Anchorage. She was a social worker for them.

This was in 1982 and 1983. Then I worked in commercial construction and I worked commercial fishing jobs. I worked anything that had an odd schedule because I started to accumulate dogs and started to race my own dogs. So I needed jobs where I could work really hard, long hours for a couple of days a week and then take the rest of the week off, or work all summer and have the winters off. So I bounced around doing all kinds of typical Alaskan jobs, construction and commercial fishing.

One of my epiphanies came while I was watching the Anchorage Fur Rendezvous. I remember the day, it was a Saturday, the second day of the Rendezvous. In those days the race was covered mile by mile by something like thirteen different television cameras. The best spot to watch was really in front of your TV with the sound turned down and the radio reporting. So I had a routine of how to watch the dog races.

The second day was the best to see the start, to go out to Tudor Track, the crossing there and then to come back to the finish. The third day was the best on TV. Anyway, I saw that the dogs, those Alaskan huskies—in those days they were called hounds—came across the finish line like flying trotters, with a diagonal displacing gait, a relatively slow gait for speed dogs, but flying meaning the dog was suspended in air. This one dog had that trotting motion, but was literally suspended in air as he crossed the finish line. I noticed a lot of those dogs were doing that. Of course the trot is the preferred gait, or was the preferred gait at the time, for sure for long-distance racing. When I saw that dog doing fifteen miles per hour or sixteen miles per hour something clicked. From then on I started breeding what I call Rendezvous dogs. Most people call them sprint dogs, but I think that's a misnomer. I call it speed racing.

Better terminology would be speed versus distance because you can't sprint twenty-five miles. But the point was that people like George Attla and Gareth Wright had done decades of genetic research, selective breeding and targeted breeding with all kinds of dogs and evolved a breed we now commonly call the Alaskan husky. They had worked on that for decades and won all of those Rendezvous and North American races and that's what I wanted. I wanted those bloodlines and so I went to those guys. I went to George

Attla, who had won the Rendezvous ten times, and I said, "Hey, here's the deal, George. I'll raise a bunch of puppies for you and I'll give you back the fastest half."

It was perfect, a win-win deal for George because he only was interested in the fastest half anyway. Whereas I was not necessarily interested in the fastest half nearly as much as I was interested in the genetics. So I did deals like that with various people, George Attla, Gareth Wright, and Jim Welch and other people who were in the "in crowd" during those years of the Rendezvous. Then, if you fast forward to the early 1990s, by then I had done enough of my own breeding and raising puppies that got me a genetic advantage over my competitors in the Iditarod.

I didn't race again in the Iditarod until 1986. And for me the watershed year was 1991. That was an unbelievable year. It changed a lot of people's lives from the front of the pack to the back. Rick Swenson won his fifth Iditarod that year, but before the race began everyone thought Susan Butcher would win her fifth Iditarod to set the record.

She was ahead leaving White Mountain and then we had that big storm and she and some other mushers turned back to wait it out. [The worst weather of the 1991 race occurred near the end, between White Mountain and Nome over the last seventy-seven miles of the trail. The temperature was approximately minus twenty-five, and a blizzard roared in from the Bering Sea with winds of about fifty miles per hour. Mushers faced frostbite and virtually no visibility.] Rick went through the storm and I chased him. That's how I finished second. I tell everybody that I learned how to win in the 1990s.

Some people were so freaked out in that storm along the coast that they never came back. They never ran another race again because it was pretty impressive. It was a game changer, all right, and of course if you're talking about championships, it totally turned Susan Butcher's life upside down. It turned Rick Swenson's life around, too. It was wild.

I'll always remember that race for being in it. I almost had a head-on collision with three mushers. I have told the story lots of times where out of this storm Susan materializes and yells at me that it can't be done, that it's too dangerous. Swenson is freezing his hands off up there. He lost his headlamp. Susan, Tim Osmar, and Joe Runyan are going back because it can't be done. They turned back to White Mountain.

I kept going. You put years into the Iditarod and you have a storm like this that makes it harder. I think while it is happening, it's kind of like raising kids. While it's happening you don't even know how big of a job it is until you have a little breathing room and you can reflect upon it. I mean right now, four championships later, and twenty-some years later, you can start thinking about it and you wonder how in the world does anybody ever win a race.

Somebody has to every year, but the complexities, how difficult it is to win that race is almost incomprehensible. Then, when you finally do it, in 1992 in my case, hey, it's pretty cool. I won again in 1994. How did that happen? It's pretty neat to think back on it in that frame of thought.

The 2002 race was pretty special, a record year. The first sub-niner. In the long run we compare that to the first four-minute mile. Everybody knows Roger Bannister broke the four-minute mile and a lot of sports followers will know that. Most sports followers don't know that Roger Bannister only had that record for a few weeks. His time has been bested over the years by about fifteen seconds, but it's always a first. It's always that he is the one that broke the four-minute mile. And in Iditarod lore I'm always gonna be the one that broke the nine-day barrier. In my case the record stood for almost ten years. That was the year I was sworn in as a US citizen. We started it in Anchorage and finished it in Nome. So for years I say I had the fastest Iditarod and the slowest swearing-in ceremony.

Before the Iditarod started the Immigration and Naturalization Service people met me in Anchorage to start the process. Then I put the paperwork and my little American flag into my sled and carried them to Nome. I called up the late Senator Ted Stevens and told him what I wanted to do and Uncle Ted helped, though I didn't need much help. My citizenship plan dated back to 9/11—September 11, 2001, when the terrorists attacked. That's what prompted me to become an American. There was not the need for anything but for me to prove to my family that this was the soil I wanted to be on and would defend. So I said, "Senator Stevens, can you give me a hand?" He said, "What legislation do you need me to enact?" I said, "A simple letter of recommendation would suffice." Long story short, we started the ceremony in private with a few individuals in downtown Anchorage and I carried that little flag all the way to the finish line. Then Nikolai, my oldest son, met me just before the finish line with a big American flag and I carried that across the finish line. Of course a judge from Nome did the swearing-in ceremony under the burled arch.

Actually, it wasn't done until a couple of days later when we got the paperwork finished. As far as I know there still hasn't been a slower swearing-in ceremony. I think that record will stand forever. But what a lot of people don't know is that we had a trifecta. I won the race, was sworn in, and then I took a thorough victory lap. We took the big American flag that Nikolai met me with and flew it on the back of a snowmobile as we drove home. Kathy, Nikolai, Rohn, and I all rode home to Big Lake that way. Friends had taken our snowmobiles to Nome on a father-daughter trip and then we took them back to Big Lake. We stopped in all of the villages. It was a big celebration. It really made the two-part celebration, already an incredible experience, into an even more incredible experience. We got halfway between Koyuk and Shaktoolik and people were already waiting for us. They heard we were on the way and they saw me flying my big American flag. People escorted us into Shaktoolik and invited us to spend the night.

I had made friends on the trail over the years and they got wind that Martin's now an American. It was just so awesome. When we got to Shaktoolik some people told us they had a nephew in Nikolai and could we take some whale meat to him. You know how the Bush pipeline works. We were chaperoned all of the way from Nome to Big Lake. It was such a great experience. We should have spent a month doing it instead of a week because we literally could have stayed anywhere we stopped. It was such a big celebration. It was really, really cool. In our family we call it the trifecta. The championship, citizenship, and the trip were all planned independently of each other. I didn't know I was going to win the Iditarod. I was going to get naturalized as a citizen, but not necessarily as the champion. And we were going to drive home from Nome on snowmobiles. If 1991 was the perfect negative storm, in 2002 it was the perfect positive storm.

People ask me, "What's your favorite victory?" I always say, "The next one." They're all pretty special, but it was just unreal when you reflect on it, how things unfolded in 2002. It's going to be hard to top 2002. But if I win another one as a fifty-six-year-old or something, setting the record for the oldest winner, that would be pretty special. It certainly could happen. Mitch Seavey won in 2013 when he was fifty-three. In dog racing that's a pretty good indicator that it could happen.

Norman Vaughan was pretty old when he was racing. Joe Redington Sr. came in fifth when he was in his seventies. I think Joe was seventy-three and he led the Iditarod. We were sitting back in Kaltag behind him chuckling and thinking that was pretty darned cool. There was no trail and there is Joe Redington Sr. in his seventies leading the Iditarod. He snuck out of Kaltag hoping to win the Iditarod. He was probably chuckling to himself.

So there is no age limit on being competitive, I don't think. You've only seen it all when you decide you have had enough. If you think you've seen it all, then you're not competitive anymore. Then you're arrogant and you're going to get beat by somebody that's open-minded enough to realize that they haven't seen it all. If you're stupid enough to think you've got it figured out, there's no such thing.

Getting ready for the Iditarod is the fun. Doing it is a grind. I think the Iditarod is probably like giving birth. Really, it's not very much fun. The pain is so bad when it's happening that you say you're never going to do it again, but getting ready for it, practicing, and all that stuff that goes around is pretty much fun. But there is a moment in the process where it's really not a lot of fun. It's what I call deep body ache, deep bone ache, the physical and mental fatigue that I don't think most people can even comprehend. They say, "I'm tired. I haven't slept in a day or two." But they've never been on the Iditarod Trail. They've never been bone tired where everything hurts, where everything is so disorganized in your biorhythms and your physical being and your mental being that parts and pieces start flying loose, like they were not even attached.

I really haven't met anybody other than people who have been in various wars that were that vulnerable, so exposed as we are on the Iditarod Trail. It's very, very hard to relay that. I don't think it's just me. I think it's where you try so hard to be competitive you've just got to go out there and push that hard, physically and mentally, that it can be a pretty dark time. Most people never get there, so it's really hard to talk about it, to explain exactly what it takes or what it feels like.

That feeling usually starts in Unalakleet or Shaktoolik, but then, very much like childbirth, the pain goes away and miraculously you do it again.

It has been suggested that it might be like someone who is climbing Mount Everest, but I don't think so. They have the oxygen debt, and air deprivation is pretty bad, but they don't have the sleep deprivation and they are not in a hurry. See, that's the thing, the mental pressure of always being in a hurry. There have been some Everest climbers who have tried to run the

Iditarod and failed in the process. There was one woman who tried a year or two ago and she was just going to check the Iditarod off her to-do list. Since she climbed Everest she thought, *What could be harder?* She didn't get to the finish line. Oops. She probably thought, *I've done Everest, I can do the Iditarod.* Well, this is a whole different animal. It might not be twenty-nine-thousand-feet high, but it's more challenging. The numbers bear that out. Way more people have climbed Everest than have done the Iditarod, by thousands.

It costs a fortune to do and there are some people who only enter the Iditarod because it is the Mount Everest of dog mushing. Some people have a different motivation, too, of just trying to do it once, not because they are dog nuts like some of us who do it thirteen years, or twenty years, in a row. I strayed away from becoming a horticulturist. I became, with Rick Swenson, and DeeDee Jonrowe and some others, the first generation who chose to be dog mushers as a profession, as a career. A Joe Redington or a Joe May never tried to make it a livelihood. They ran it because it was a cool event. We're trying to run it and make a business out of it, a lifestyle, a vocation, a career.

So it's a different ballgame. The next generation, the ones that are up and coming, the young Seaveys, or the young Busers, or the Jake Berkowit-zes, or Pete Kaisers, they have a previous generation to draw from, get experience from on how to do it. We didn't have that. We didn't have professional long-distance racers to try to pick their brains. Whereas now we know, it's an established, yet difficult path, but it can be done.

Now I'm just about as busy in the summer as I am in the winter. I train the dogs in the winter, but I entertain tourists in the summer. They come to my dog lot and I give them a show. From my exit interviews talking to the people what I see is what they really appreciate about being here. They love the dog stories, sharing the lifestyle, the experience, how we care for the dogs. They had never put thought behind what we do with the dogs on a year-round basis.

We started out small, like everything, with just a few special interest groups visiting. Tour organizers began bringing small groups on an organized basis. They had people who wanted to see how an Iditarod dog-sled operation worked behind the scenes. Now the tour has grown and it's five stages. We have a visitors center building and buses come in. We introduce them to a bunch of sled dogs and provide information. We try to set the record straight about the dogs and fix any misconceptions. Everybody expects to see the Siberian huskies, the photogenic huskies that we insult by calling "Sloberians." We introduce people to the Alaskan huskies. We tell them it's a little bit like the difference between Clydesdales and the Kentucky Derby winner.

Part of the information we give them is what it takes for a dog to run a marathon, what it takes to run 150 miles in a twenty-four-hour period. I tell them the color of their eyes doesn't matter and that not all of them have as much hair as they might think. They don't run with their eyes and I don't really care what color they are—they could be polka-dotted. The dogs are sixty-pound dogs with one-hundred-pound hearts. The mongrel breed are eternal children. By the time we walk away from the dogs they know a lot about the breed.

We go into the trophy room and then do a little multimedia presentation by the log amphitheater. I talk about what I call thirty attributes in a good sled dog. By then the tourists know that speed, endurance, and leadership are some of the things we look for. In the movie they learn that the dogs metabolize up to eleven thousand calories in a day on the Iditarod, so they understand why being a good eater is important.

They hear that the dogs take two million steps in the Iditarod. One day I was bored on the Iditarod Trail and I measured the stride and counted how many steps the dogs take. That's eight million opportunities to get a cut, abrasion, broken toenail, or something else for each dog. So it's really amazing that they even get there. Then people get to interact with the puppies and we hook up six or seven dogs and run them around the perimeter of the dog yard. We don't give rides, but when people leave they should know a whole lot more about sled dogs.

I still have things I'd like to do in the Iditarod. I absolutely still think of myself as a contender. I go into the race every year with the idea that I can win it. I contemplate all of the time how nice it would be to get one more. I also contemplate that when I'm in my seventies how cool it would be to run the Iditarod and not have to race. I think of Skwentna or Finger Lake or Rainy Pass where I probably spend two hours there on a yearly basis. If I could double or triple the time I spent there it would feel like a vacation. I could camp my way up the Bering Sea Coast and still not finish last because of experience. In a way I am looking forward to that happening a couple of decades from now, just to travel the trail to do it. That would be a lot of fun.

I wouldn't need ninety dogs in my kennel as reserves, either. I could just take a bunch of dogs and go up the trail. If it got a little cold or a little hot or I got a little tired, I could sleep a little more. But I'd be there. I'd get there to Nome. I'll be on the trail and finish the race and hopefully continue my by-then unprecedented finishing streak of twenty-eight in a row.

I tell everybody that unless I find something to replace the passion that I have for my dogs and my lifestyle and my whole Alaska existence I'm not going to change. If something comes along like collecting postage stamps, or whatever, if that fascinates me as much as dogs, then I might change. To fly as a pilot, or bike on a motorcycle, or golf, those are some things I don't do because I might like them too much. I don't even want to try.

I did the math and I think I'll be seventy-five when I do my fiftieth Iditarod. I just live with my dogs and live with my lifestyle and I very much enjoy what I'm doing.

CHAPTER 2

Jeff
KING

Probably the winningest long-distance musher across the board, Jeff King is a four-time Iditarod champion who has shown no sign of slowing down after more than thirty years in the sport. Except for bad luck in the final thirty miles of the 2014 race King would have claimed his fifth crown. King lives in Denali Park, Alaska, on the outskirts of Denali National Park, far removed from his California roots where he grew up as a high school wrestling competitor.

King first ran the Iditarod in 1981, but became a more avid competitor in the early 1990s after he had claimed victory in the one-thousand-mile Yukon Quest in 1989. He recorded his first Iditarod triumph in 1993, his second in 1996, his third in 1998, and his fourth in 2006. Although King said he was retiring when he skipped the 2011 race, he did not stay away from the Iditarod for long.

In addition to being a four-time title-holder, King owns nine other finishes in the top three. Among King's other Iditarod honors are winning the Humanitarian Award twice, capturing the Spirit of Alaska Award twice, and the Joe Redington Sr. Award once. King has also been viewed as a training innovator, experimenting with new methods of preparing his huskies for races. He believes that mushers are still learning what the dogs are capable of doing.

Besides making his mark in the Iditarod, King has been the king of the Kuskokwim 300 in Bethel, winning that prestigious event nine times. He has also won the Copper Basin 300 twice and the International Rocky Mountain Stage Stop Race in Wyoming.

When I was a kid I read Jack London's books and that helped get me interested in the north. I always liked the outdoors and I always liked dogs. I was in California, but I was never a kid who liked to go to the beach. There was a place that had guide dogs for the blind near us and then we moved right next door to Jack London State Park. So, yeah, I kind of had my eye on the north.

In college I thought the panhandle of Idaho was where I was going to live, on the Snake River. Then I looked at the map and looked a little higher and thought there was another place. When I first became aware of sled dogs I thought, *Oh, they're transportation. This is fundamental, back-to-nature transportation.* It was more related to subsistence. I wanted to live out a childhood dream, living in a tent, trapping and using dogs for transportation, hunting, and fishing.

The first mushing I did was taking backcountry trips with my neighbor Bruce Lee. He lived near me and he was training to race. I just went with him for fun. One day, checking my mail at the post office, I saw a handwritten flyer advertising a little race in Healy and I thought, *That sounds like fun. I'll meet some other mushers.*

The next thing I know I'm a racer. I think I've done twenty-three Iditarods and seven Yukon Quests and I'm still going in my late fifties. I never expected to still be racing at this age. My ex-wife, Donna, reminded me that I once said, "If we're still doing this at forty, somebody just take us out back and whup on us." I'm not retiring now. On the contrary, I'm having a blast. I have a good enough cash flow. It isn't as precarious to get to a race and figure out how I'm gonna make it.

Going into the 2014 race I planned to have more miles on my dog team than at any time in my life. I've got a rig with tracks on it and I've been training by truck for a long time now. It's a Jeep Wrangler and was my birthday present to myself. It's got a CD player and a heater and a trailer full of booties for dogs. I stand my ground with anyone who thinks it's being a sissy. We can do things we never could before. I can train thirty dogs at a time.

I can stop the dogs anytime and keep them stopped. I can figure, "This is where they should rest." If you're on a sled you just can't stop like that. Some people, like Ramey Smyth, are willing to shiver around a smoky willow fire, but day after day for months at a time? I'm here to tell you that the sport has not yet gotten the dogs to their best condition at the start of the Iditarod. I'm positive of it. When Lance Mackey won the Yukon Quest and then went right to the Iditarod, everybody said it couldn't be done, including me: "Oh, it's ridiculous." We thought it was such a fluke that it would never happen again. And of course it happened again and again, and then other people did it.

One thing that made an impact on me, from my own experience, is that when I ran the Kobuk 440 for the first time in the late 1980s, I was sitting around with my idols of yesteryear, Susan Butcher and Rick Swenson, and I was listening to them and absorbing what they said like a sponge. They were talking about how amazing it was that the dogs had so much energy for those April spring races. It was like they could go forever. They were openly talking about how they had come from the Iditarod and the dogs weren't tired, but maybe stronger. One of them had just won the Iditarod and that was telling me the dogs hadn't reached their peak yet.

In 2008, we had the All Alaska Sweepstakes race to commemorate the original one and Lance Mackey, Mitch Seavey, and I were just coming off the Iditarod. I only had one dog in my team that did not finish the Iditarod. I had fresh dogs at home, but I didn't have confidence in them. We didn't drop dogs and we blew like sixteen hours off the records of Leonhard Seppala, Iron Man Johnson, and Rick Swenson from 1982. It was like, "What the hell's going on?" In 2013, I had an outstanding Iditarod and I went to the Kobuk 440. I felt great. I was coming home after that and they were in better shape. What's the deal?

My point is that I don't think we're there yet in understanding what the dogs can do. It's like my training in the jeep. I'm sitting back there in comfort and I wonder, *Why has no one done this?* I don't know. I may find out it's the wrong idea, but I don't think so. I just think it's another thing we haven't tried. If you think you can train a dog team on a four-wheeler or on a sled as well as I can train thirty dogs while being warm and well fed, watching them all at the same time instead of trying to learn from what your handler tells you about how the other team did, well. . . . On a sled it's just so hard to do. Sometimes you go, "What the hell." You're cold and sometimes they just want to go, so you go. It's not in their best interest for conditioning.

I'm excited by the fact that I don't think we've really nailed this. I think we're on the cusp of learning something new, that the dogs have not done yet. I got a whole month ahead in training. What I am doing that no one does in training is that consistent slow run series, what running the Iditarod and Quest does for the dogs. It's doing never more than six hours and emulating the twenty-four-hour break. When Lance won the Quest and the Iditarod I recognized there was a benefit, but I thought I could make it even better without being in a race.

The idea was to adjust the training to duplicate some of that racing, but instead of dropping a dog, I'm going to carry it and give it a day off and then put it back in the team. I'll build a team rather than being in a race and be influenced by the trail, the remoteness of the trail, and the challenges of caring for a dog team while you're tired, which is what people have to do when they're in a race.

I can care for them better and mimic the schedule of running. I personally wouldn't do it if I just stood on the back of a sled. I've been there a lot. I'm not ashamed to tell you that it gets to a point where so many thousand miles a year is enough. The rest of my energy I want to put in in a way that I can make me a better dog-care administrator and better strategist, where I'm not influenced by, "Well, I'm freezing my ass off again" or "This sled is not carrying enough food" or "This dog needs to be carried" or whatever the case may be. I take my own weaknesses out of the equation of training. That's the bottom line.

I do believe I can win the Iditarod again, even if I would be the oldest one to do it. I was so close in 2013 [third]. I made some mistakes that kept me from winning and I never in my career felt, *Wow, if I had just done this or that.* A couple of key things I screwed up. If you win the Kusko and you win the Kobuk, you've got the team that can win the Iditarod. It's one of the things that demonstrates you're capable. Statistics and history show it.

When I go back to my first Iditarod victory in 1993 it was a three-person race between me, DeeDee Jonrowe, and Rick Mackey. We were all way more physical mushers and our physical effort on the sled was greater because our dogs were slower and we didn't know the things we know now. I think we go faster now with less effort physically because we know how to do it so much better. I have memories of passing Rick at the Old Woman cabin and realizing, *Wow, I can win this thing. I can do this.* Jim Leach was the veterinarian and he really boosted my ego when he said, "Jeff, your dogs look great." If you hear that from the head vet, it's hard to do anything, but just do backflips.

It was really close between me and DeeDee. The lead was just seven minutes at White Mountain. It was at White Mountain that I put my two leaders, Kitty and Herbie, together for the first time. They had both been fantastic. But early in the race I thought they were going to run my team into the ground. I realized those guys wanted to go, but I was scared to put them together because the rest of the team just couldn't keep up with them. Then I put them together and we had either the winner's fastest time from White Mountain or the fastest time anyone had gone.

On the way in to the finish line I remember listening to KNOM radio and hearing someone in the spotter vehicle exclaim about how fast I was going. I heard this guy going, "Oh, my God, this team is loping down the beach." I'm thinking, *You're damned right, it is!* It was really a wonderful moment, one of my favorites. To listen to the radio and have them describe to me how my team looked was pretty special.

Another thing that was so special was the influence of C. J. Kolbe. He had cancer and got a ride with me at the start and he gave me a lucky penny. That victory was so special and memorable because of him. All of the wins have been tremendously satisfying—they've been similar that way.

My last victory in 2006 stands out because it was so superior. I went down Front Street with fourteen dogs doing fifteen miles per hour. Looking at the film from that overhead camera and seeing my dogs lope going down the street is one of the best memories I've ever had. I get to watch it over and over again because it's been recorded on film. I remember it so well. One of the other years, my daughter Ellen, my youngest, rode the sled in with me while drinking a Pepsi.

When I was saying those things about not being in the Iditarod when I was forty or fifty, it just seemed irresponsible to expect to be doing something like this forever. It's supposed to be a hobby for just so long. It turned into my career. In the beginning I was always broke. It's a hobby when you can't pay for it. Golf is a hobby right up until somebody pays you a million bucks to put their Nike swoosh on your hat. If you can make a living playing poker, then you're a professional poker player. The rest of us play for matches.

I'm absolutely blessed because what I do is more fun than not. I love the variation in my year, too, that I don't have the same thing going on month to month. There are some seasons. Today I was on heavy equipment. Yesterday I was mushing dogs. Tomorrow I'll be mushing dogs and Sunday night I'm going to Fairbanks and going out to a movie and dinner. I often ask myself, and others who are in a similar situation, I hope we are appreciating this enough because we are very lucky people.

I feel like I'm going to keep going. I'm fifty-eight, but my body is holding up. I don't know if it's in my future to keep racing if I don't think I can win or be a contender. What is more likely is that if I don't have a contending team, or my body and preparation is not good enough, if I stay with the Iditarod it will be as a mentor of somebody very specific. I'm not even going to say anymore how long I'll be doing this. I'll do it if it is still fun.

One thing I get a giant kick out of is my summer business. Between May 15 and September 15 I get tour buses full of people who visit the dog yard. I had about twenty-five-thousand people come through in the summer of 2013. That's a season.

The people are greeted with a puppy and get photos and then we have presenters. I am one of those. The other presenter is a skilled public speaker who can make people laugh and who understands the Alaska lifestyle. We tell them things about dogs and the origins of sled dogs and racing and we hitch up dogs to a four-wheeler. We don't give rides, but they see the excitement when dogs are hitched up. They feel it. We have other training apparatus. I have a dog in a large hamster wheel that just goes like hell. Then I give an indoor presentation. We have a theater building. I've got thirty-five years of trophies in there and bear skins on the walls. It lasts about two and a half hours. I do it three times a day, seven days a week in the summer.

It is quite a pace, but I look forward to it. It's not just about me, but I am kind of the core of the story to some degree. My youngest daughter is awesome. She and my girlfriend are awesome presenters. I've had Shawn Sidelinger, a five-time Iditarod veteran, doing it. We have been the number one rated attraction on Trip Advisor for Denali Park. We are five-star rated for customer satisfaction, so we're doing something right. People say it feels authentic to them. I've been doing it for twenty years now. We've got a knack for it and there's a market for it with visitors. They really love it. I think what we are is part of the romance of Alaska.

We consistently have people tell us that this is the best thing they did on their trip from the moment they left their house until they got home and I think in general they like their trips. I'm totally flattered and all it does is make me want to do better. I'm not sure if I ever envisioned myself in this role exactly, but when I was in first grade I brought my race-car bedspread to school, spread it out over some desks, and sang "Hot Rod Lincoln" to my class. I was going to be a comedian. I was so in love with Bill Cosby and the Smothers Brothers that I aspired to be a comedian. As a little kid I loved performing. I didn't know what I was going to do, but I was absolutely a ham.

The fact is I do clearly have a knack for performing and public speaking on dog mushing. There are certain audiences that by demographics are more likely to enjoy what you do. And we've found that niche. Those are the people who are coming here because they absolutely love it. They are the target audience. I don't think they are necessarily coming because it is Jeff King. They know the Iditarod is a sled-dog race, but I don't know if they all know my name. They're told, "You've heard of the Iditarod? Well, Jeff King has won it four times. This is a homestead we'll be going to." So they've heard of the Iditarod and they've heard of dog mushing and now they know there's a four-time champion named Jeff King who they are going to see.

It's not all about the Iditarod. I've probably done every race in the state. One of the things I'm proudest of is that I've never had a fatality in my team. I've won the Humanitarian Award multiple times. In the Sweepstakes you can't even drop a dog. We took sixteen hours off the record. It can be done. You need to raise the bar. I may have a fatality someday while I'm mushing dogs, but I'm ahead of the norm, proof that it is way more than a rarity than it has been to date.

The Iditarod is so much better known than when I first ran it in 1981. The Internet is huge. There are millions of hits on the Iditarod site, though I do wonder how many users there are. There's a really committed group that gets totally addicted to it. I think nobody outside of Alaska knew about the Iditarod until a woman [Libby Riddles and Susan Butcher] won a couple of times. That was huge and in my opinion a selling point. Nobody cared about guys running sled dogs across Alaska until a woman beat everybody and then did it again and again. They didn't know it wasn't the same person. Susan Butcher's dominance catapulted the race into continental North America, if not global perception. I don't think it would be anywhere near where it is today without that tremendous booster rocket in marketing.

There's not a person that comes to this facility who doesn't remember Susan Butcher. People said, "I talked to her" and "I read about her." As much as I loved what Susan did for the race, Libby's been horribly shortchanged [as the first female winner in 1985]. Susan was good for the race. She had enough personality and presence that she was very fun for the dog-mushing world to show off. She was attractive and well-spoken and tough and feminine all in one.

I continue to be fascinated by how many people want to try sled-dog racing. The Knik 200 opened for signups and hit its maximum number of forty teams in twenty-four hours and there's a waiting list. The allure is bigger than ever. I went out to help a young couple that worked for me for a couple of years, bought land, bought a few dogs from me a few years ago, and now they've got nineteen and they're going to run their first races. They're a young couple and they're going to town to spend $2,400 for a pallet of dog food. They're eating beans and have no electricity, but are spending $2,400 for a pallet of dog food to last two months. It's all they want to do, run the dogs. They find it rewarding.

Every year I bring a sense of excitement to the starting line of the Iditarod. It's no longer nauseatingly nervous. It was for many, many years. I'm not sure it helped me win, and I think it can be a hindrance. I actually think eventually not feeling like I have to win might make it easier to win. If you push too hard—I look back and go, *Wow, I should have done this and that and I should have backed off a little bit and I would have done better.* I don't know if I'm a mellow Jeff King, but I am certainly mellower than I was. Some years ago, Al Marble, a race judge in Shaktoolik, said, "You're not the same Jeff King I remember." In my mind I remember thinking, *Man, you're so much more relaxed than you used to be.*

It would mean a lot to me to win a fifth Iditarod. If anything, in 2013, I was trying too hard. I honestly think the fun part for me is I know that you can do it with a team that you're just beaming proud of. People have gone as hard as they could as long as they could and it doesn't get you there before somebody else. Thank God we know that now. It is experience.

The human body can't stay awake for nine straight days, but you can be "checked out," as I like to call it, on the sled. Taking care of the dogs becomes more routine and quicker and easier that in some ways I feel like I get as much sleep, or more sleep, than I ever did. It's closer to four hours a day. I target three hours and two ninety-minute naps. I know if the dogs run fifteen hours they need to rest nine. I can care for those dogs in three hours, leaving me six hours to sleep and eat. There are fewer and fewer dogs that need things more than the others do. In most cases it's just food and water. Sometimes you stop, they hit the deck, eat, and go to sleep. And I'm done. I hit the deck and go to sleep. I get up and go for another nine hours. All you have to do is stay awake and keep from freezing your ass off for nine hours.

The dogs are just incredible. It continues to amaze me what they can do. I think that's probably one of the most significant things that are different in the Iditarod over the years—the dogs are way better.

Dog Ma, official Iditarod poster, 2009.

CHAPTER 3

Dan
SEAVEY

etired Seward, Alaska, schoolteacher Dan Seavey is one of the grand old men of the Iditarod. He was there at the beginning in 1973, helping Joe Redington Sr. get the one-thousand-mile race going, and he lives on vicariously these days through other members of the family who keep the long-distance sled-dog racing tradition strong.

Dan Seavey placed third in the first Iditarod, winning $6,000. But aware that the race's finances were shaky he generously delayed accepting his prize money. Forevermore a strong booster of the race, the Seavey clan's patriarch, who moved north to Alaska from Minnesota with his wife in the early 1960s, competed seriously in the Iditarod in 1973 and 1974 and only once in a great while since. He entered in 1997 for old time's sake and later competed one more time in his seventies so that three generations of Seaveys could leave the starting line in one race.

A strong backer of Iditarod Trail preservation, Dan Seavey glowed with pride as his son Mitch won his first Iditarod championship in 2004 and then as grandson Dallas won the race in 2012. In 2013, father bested son as Mitch won a second crown.

Seward is a seaport town located on Resurrection Bay on the Kenai

Peninsula. The city was named after William Seward, the US secretary of state under President Abraham Lincoln. Hemmed in by mountains, the community of about three thousand people is at mile 0 of the Iditarod Trail. The National Historic Trail was established in Seward in order for supplies to be transported overland into the Interior for gold miners.

Seward is not a part of the Iditarod Trail where the mushers race, but Dan Seavey is devoted to keeping the memory of his home portion of the trail alive.

My initial interest in the race was not as a race at all because there was no race when I first came to Seward. My wife and I came from north central Minnesota. We arrived in August of 1963 and I had a teaching job at Seward High School. It was basically social studies, but the curriculum included history and part of that was a semester of Alaska history for seniors. Of course I was interested in Alaska history to start with otherwise I wouldn't have been here. I had read up a lot on the history before I moved. So it didn't take me long to realize that Seward was connected in a big way to the historic Iditarod Trail.

My interest started with Seward's position and importance to the trail. Coupled with that bookish interest in the history of the trail was the dog-mushing part of it. My dog-mushing interest—and you have probably heard this from more than one person of my vintage—started with Sergeant Preston and the Northwest Mounted Police on the radio. We'd get the chores done by six or seven o'clock, whenever it came on. You didn't want to miss one adventure. So there was this concept, this kid-ish dream of mushing dogs. We weren't in Seward more than a month and we already got a husky. It wasn't a sled dog, but it looked as if it could be if it knew how to be. By the time the first Iditarod rolled around I had nine or ten years of experience on the runners. There was a huge learning curve that takes place. You had to know how to manage a dog team.

It was all recreational riding around the area, but darn it I never got a badge like Sergeant Preston and I never caught a bad guy. My leaders never came up to the Yukon King standard, but I did have the background with dogs and dog mushing and that led to my association with the Aurora Dog

Mushers and Joe Redington. We'd go to Anchorage for the sprint races and prior to the race everyone would talk and that's where the hatching of the long-distance race took place. Of course in 1967 they had that Alaska centennial purchase race out of Knik. That planted the seed.

Once that race happened, though, for most people the Iditarod was a dead issue. The exception was a few key people, not the least being Joe Redington and Dorothy Page. Bill Cotter, myself, Dave Olson, and a few others took an interest. We ran our dogs in the Saturday and Sunday afternoon races and then we'd sit around till dark drinking coffee and talking about the big one, the real Iditarod, not a fifty-miler. So I was basically in on the ground floor of the first Iditarod and the planning up to a point. Somewhere along the way I decided I wanted to run this race and I started backing off from the planning.

As far as the attitude toward long-distance mushing at the time, of course we had doubting Thomases even in our own ranks. There was a lot of talk about the trail and going to Iditarod, but Iditarod was a ghost town and nobody would see you leave and nobody would see you come in. Anchorage became a natural for the starting point. Nome was decided on for the finish, which lengthened not only the race, but our whole idea of logistics, checkpoints, and all the things that are necessary. We basically doubled the distance deciding on Nome.

Everyone knew Nome from the Gold Rush, and the logistical support was there. There was commercial airline service and so forth and all that was really important. Nome may not be the best place to end an international sporting event, but it's tradition now.

I started the race with twelve dogs and I was carrying 250 pounds on the sled, not counting me. There was also a provision for dog food to be dropped off in five different places along the way. Some of the places were McGrath and Unalakleet, but you had to scramble to get to Nome in that first race. A lot of the logistics fell apart. If they were ever all in place they didn't all work out and there were times that we were literally lost without food for dogs and people.

Being in that Iditarod was by far the number one adventure of my life. I've lived forty more years after that and I've done some more Iditarods, but there'll never be a first one again. It really was the adventure of my life. I can identify with the mushers who sign up who are not the professional mushers and who look at the Iditarod as being the adventure of their life. Absolutely. I can't think of any more noble reason for running it than adventure. I mean it's certainly not treasure. Even the professional mushers admit that. There's not much treasure and there's a heck of a lot of adventure and self-satisfaction that comes from completing something of that nature.

Mitch was my number one handler in both the 1973 and 1974 races. He was a twelve-and-a-half, thirteen-year-old kid, and he was one tough kid, even at that time. I think I saw it coming with Mitch that he would race the Iditarod. I think it was to be expected. We had three children. One got involved with horses and one went completely away from working with animals. One out of three is not too bad.

Mitch's children grew up with dogs, right from the start. Mitch and Janine have four sons and doing the Iditarod is sort of a rite of passage. For Danny, Tyrell, Dallas, and Conway, it's something on the order if you want to leave home you have to run the Iditarod first. But the kids love it. They grew up with it. They're home-schooled kids, self-reliant, self-sufficient, can make decisions, live with mistakes, and learn from them. I think it's been a tremendous life for those kids. I really do. I am very proud.

In 1997 I trained up a team for old time's sake because it was the twenty-fifth anniversary of the race and Tyrell was my trainer-handler. At twelve years old he said he was going to bring me into the modern era of dog mushing. He stuck with me on the trail, trained all winter, and it was so much fun. All of my equipment was archaic. Tyrell would say, "Why are you messing with those old poles you got from Army-Navy surplus? You need one of these Northern Outfitters cold-weather systems." So I shelled out $1,500 for the cold-weather system to help me, but I hadn't used it before. I cast it aside by the time I left for Nome. He just kind of shook his head, but I kind of notice in the racing since then I see a lot of layer stuff being used.

Once we were training in the Moose Range outside of Knik and it was raining. We gave the dogs a break so we could catch a couple of hours sleep. He dove into his sleeping bag and I just made a pad on the ground. We said goodnight and I was just laying there looking at the sky and I got to thinking that it was almost twenty-five years to the day, I'd bet, maybe within two days and within two blocks of the same spot that Tyrell and I were bedded down, where I had bedded down with Mitch when he was training with me. That was really an eye-opener for me. I thought, *Holy cow, how can all of those years have gone by?* And here I was with a grandson training dogs. I'll tell you, that's worth living for. It was special.

In 1997, I got back in the Iditarod because of the celebration of the anniversary. It appealed to me. I looked at it as just a sentimental journey. I was a lot closer to the front in 1973 [third] and 1974 [fifth] than I was in 1997 [thirty-fifth]. I thought I did pretty well in those first races. I had a job as a teacher and it was very difficult for me to persuade the school board that I should take two months every year to run the race.

I came in in the middle of the pack in 1997, but I make no apologies for it. I was never really considered a serious dog racer, even approaching the first race. The Iditarod for me has always been bookish, if that's what you want to call it. I've always said why let racing interfere and mess up a good activity like dog mushing. Can you think of any place where for that small an amount of money you can get support like you do to run one thousand miles like you do in the Iditarod? I mean, it's a cheap vacation.

I did the Iditarod again in 2001 and that was the three generations race. It was the first time three generations from one family had entered the Iditarod in the same year. Mitch and Danny and I raced. Danny was a rookie. The way the race played out we actually ended up on the trail together and that was pretty neat.

We called it "The Three Generations Race." I believe it was Mitch's idea. Danny was coming up through the ranks and he was going to run it as a rookie. So it became, "Why don't we all three go?" I said, "Nah." They kept going, "Come on." You know, pretty soon they had me talked into it and it was real neat because we didn't often run dogs together. Mitch had some dog-team problems that year and decided to dump the racing and drop back. From Anvik to Nome, I think, we did the whole thing together. It was great to travel with those guys and make a little history, too.

All of these years, from September of 1963 to now, I've always had a dog team and even today I'm out there with the dogs. It's a good core of dogs. I belong to the Iditarod National Historic Alliance, which is a private, non-profit organization that is concerned essentially with the history of the trail, preserving the trail, and all that might entail. And I've been president of that. I'm on the board and have been for years and years.

So 2012 was the centennial, the one hundredth anniversary of the historic trail and we worked for four years to publicize it. I got talked into doing the race again, but I wasn't competing or traveling with members of my family. We obtained a legislative citation and I delivered it to each of the villages along the way, citing them as a very important part of the history of the trail and for their support of the race. I stopped and gave a talk at each of the villages that I passed through. It wasn't always a formal talk, but often it was. For me it was like old home week.

There were still people around who remembered the first race. They had been kids at the time. In one place someone said, "Ooh, we remember when you and Bobby Vent came through on the first race and you had breakfast at my uncle's place right over there." I said, "How old were you?" He said, "Five years old." Things like that happened.

White Mountain wasn't even supposed to be a checkpoint. We were going to go right across Golovin Bay. But the people said, "You've got to stop at White Mountain." So at the last minute they decided to go through White Mountain with the race, but the problem was there was no dog food. So we had to buy fish. Howard Lake was the checker. He's an old, old man now, but he always kept track of the Seaveys. I had no more stopped in White Mountain in 2012 than here comes a great-grandson of his, maybe a great-great grandson, driving him down on a snowmachine to see me. It was tremendous. I even finished fiftieth in the race, too.

The Seaveys made history again that year. There were three generations in the race again. Dallas was running instead of Danny. The race was a lot different. I was on a different mission and Dallas and Mitch were in it to win. Dallas won the race. I was at Kaltag and I was getting ready to leave when the checker came up to me and said, "You know, Dallas is already into Nome and won the race. You want to come up to my place and watch it on television?" So I postponed my departure for about two hours. Of all things. I'm about three hundred miles behind him.

The race is so much faster now than when we started. They win in under ten days and that first race was twenty days. I do marvel at the speed. That's probably the most common question I get asked: "How is it different nowadays compared to back in the dark ages?" Obviously, it's faster and that's the bottom line. And of course the question is why. Mitch and I figured out (at that time) we had eighteen generations of dogs, of dog breeding, all aimed towards more speed. Just in our family, eighteen generations, and it's probably twenty by now.

Another question I get asked a lot is how we make the dogs run and how we make them work. The answer is, "We don't." The dogs want to run. They can't help themselves. Take a water dog, a retriever, and if you get him near water you can't keep him out of the water. So with twenty generations of dogs built for speed and endurance, you can't keep them from running. You don't make them. You, with the bigger brain and so forth, have to keep them from running themselves to death. You also have to make sure they have good nutrition.

The first dog team I got to Nome we made it on halibut bits, Purina, plus a little beef, and that was not unusual. Whatever mushers had they fed the dogs and they just fed them more of the same because that was all they had. Now, for $1.20 a pound you can get nutrition in a bag that would rival any balanced diet you could make up.

The trail is a lot different, too. It wasn't as if the trail was cleared. The army was out there a week before, but it got all blown in. Mostly, the musher was the trailbreaker. One time we were literally lost south of the trail and I went backwards for two and a half miles. I was stomping out things like the words "Dog Food" in the snow with the hope that an airplane would fly over and read it.

We piled our sleds high with equipment that first race because we didn't know what we were going to face. Over the years the race has come up with a list of things that a musher has to take, the mandatory equipment. Once, several years ago Bill Cotter—when he had run nineteen Iditarods—told me he had never taken his snowshoes out on the trail. He said, "Well, I think they're in the bottom of the sled there somewhere."

We took plenty of stuff in the beginning that we might use. It was definitely a pioneering effort. We didn't know what the Iditarod would become, but I think everyone who did that first one was glad he did. Dick Mackey, a very good friend, was vacillating about entering the first race. "Should I go, or shouldn't I?" I said, "Dick, look at it this way: There'll never be another first, I don't care if there's a thousand more. There will never be another first one and you'd be an Iditarod race pioneer. There's no race on earth, there never was, of this dimension, and there may never be a second one."

A lot of things during that race could have put the kibosh on the whole works. Bear Creek Mine, owned by Tex Gates, way over in Placerville, wasn't intended to be a checkpoint, but somehow we got lost and ended up at his mine, and he pulled out his shotgun and said, "Go away." But a big blizzard hit and it turned out he accommodated us. Who knows? If he hadn't we might still be out there.

Many guys helped me, helped us, out there, a lot of volunteers—and it wasn't all a male show, either—did yeoman service. They helped get us through that country and over that trail. Every one of them is a pioneer, too.

CHAPTER 4

Mitch
SEAVEY

itch Seavey grew up around Alaska huskies, working with the dogs in his father Dan's kennel from the time he was a youngster. His father said it was virtually preordained that at some point Mitch would compete in the Iditarod.

Although in retrospect that seems to be the case, Mitch Seavey's long-distance mushing career has not been a straight line. The younger Seavey, who grew up in Seward, Alaska, and now lives in Sterling, made his debut in the Iditarod in 1982 with a very respectable twenty-second-place finish. However, after that race he stepped off the sled runners for years, focusing on other things in life.

Mitch Seavey did not return to Iditarod competition until 1995. Since then he has been an Iditarod regular and become a two-time champion and a perpetual title contender. Seavey won the one-thousand-mile contest for the first time in 2004 and repeated in 2013. When Mitch Seavey captured the title in 2013 at age fifty-three he became the oldest musher to win the world's most prestigious dog-sled race. A year later he finished third.

Three Seavey sons, Tyrell, Danny, and Dallas, have raced in the Iditarod and his fourth son, Conway, has been a Junior Iditarod competitor and is seen as a sure bet to try the long race when he is old enough. Dallas won the 2012 championship and in 2013, with his fourth-place finish, was one of the top mushers who helped chase his father to the finish line. In 2005 Dallas Seavey was the youngest musher to ever enter the Iditarod, turning eighteen the day before the start of the race. He was also a national caliber high school wrestler.

The 2014 Iditarod was Mitch Seavey's twenty-first race and unlike in other sports where athletes are considered over the hill at forty, he believes he is just improving with age.

I definitely first got involved with dog mushing because it was in the family. I was around my dad Dan's dogs a lot and I sensed it was going to be something important in my life, too. I felt from very early on that my Iditarod mushing experiences were just beginning when I helped my dad train.

My dad was part of the Iditarod beginnings and so from a very young age my boyhood dream was to win the Iditarod. We could mush on trails right near our home, whether it was for three miles or ten miles and I was going along fantasizing about winning the Iditarod when I was mushing a three-dog team or a five-dog team. From very early on I loved mushing and I wanted to race.

In other parts of the country, maybe Indiana, boys would dream of growing up and hitting the winning shot in the seventh game of the NBA basketball championships. That's a good analogy. To me the Iditarod was the Alaska Super Bowl.

Because we lived in Alaska I also grew up with the opportunity from the background of our family. My first Iditarod was in 1982, but I had actually planned to run in the 1980 Iditarod. But the summer before that I met my wonderful bride, Janine, and that derailed the whole Iditarod plan. We got married in March instead of me doing the Iditarod that March. Of course I get no end of grief for never being around for our anniversary because I'm always on the trail. Our anniversary is March 8 and that means I'm always out on the Iditarod.

By 1982 Janine was pregnant with our first son, Danny. I ran that race and Danny was born a couple of months later and I thought at that time that was going to be my one and only Iditarod. When I raced that year I thought it was going to be just once to get it out of my system. I had a family. I wanted to do things. I was going to start a career and what not. So I didn't run the Iditarod again for thirteen years.

The next Iditarod I ran was in 1995. And then all the years I ran we had small children. We were busy and out of state some of the time on business, too. Finally, when I got back to it we started our sled-dog tour business and in conjunction with that I got back into racing. It's not like it is now when a lot of people do summer dogsled tours, give rides, or make presentations.

My dad had been involved in some dogsled demonstrations, but not in giving rides. Then we started dry-land tours with rides. We were the first that I knew of, though I heard that Richard Burmeister had done some things on the beach in Nome. As part of our concept we made carts that could carry multiple people at once. The weather in Seward is especially cool and wet in the summer. It was nice for the dogs to work in without getting too hot, so it worked out really well. They're everywhere now.

When I returned to the Iditarod it wasn't just to race one more time. We jumped in up to our necks. We had a kennel. We had property. We moved where the trails were good. We were into it and I envisioned, in conjunction with the tour business, doing the race every year.

And when I got into the Iditarod again I wanted to be competitive. I am a competitive person. I was a wrestler, a college wrestler, a state champion and while I wasn't too good at it, I did run and do cross-country and other things. I was competitive minded. When I started running the Iditarod, even the first time in 1982, it didn't enter my mind to run a noncompetitive race. So I've always run thinking that I was going to try to place well, which I'm not sure is good advice for everybody. I think you need to be realistic. But since my dad had been third and fifth the two times he did it, I thought I'd be right there, too.

But almost ten years had elapsed since he raced and another thirteen years had elapsed since I did it and things had changed. You don't just fall off a turnip truck and be in the top five like the first few years when they were inventing the race.

There is much more of a learning curve now. Absolutely. Our approach has always been every year that we want to learn something more. We always ask the question, "What's going to make me better this year than last year? How am I going to be better, a better competitor than I was last year?" When I ran in 1982 I don't think I was surprised by how much I didn't know. I knew I didn't know a lot.

I really felt like a babe in the woods when I ran my rookie race, even coming from an Iditarod family. It had been almost ten years since my dad had run. We weren't really competitive. We had dogs, but there was a gap in there I was trying to fill and the information wasn't as available. We were saving newspaper clippings to see how long people stopped for rests, where they stopped, and what their run-rest schedules were. Now it's all available. You can follow all of that on a website. It took a while to learn back then. The race has speeded up, too. In 1982 it took me seventeen and a half days to finish. And I've done it in nine days.

The Iditarod has changed. It was a different world between 1982 and 1995 and it's a different world between 1995 and now. In 1982 we were snowshoeing and there was so much snow we couldn't find the trail. In 1995 it was a decent trail and you shouldn't get lost. There was an actual strategy of competition besides just surviving. There was a bigger change between 1982 and 1995 than 1995 to the present.

Times have gotten so much faster. Nine and a half days isn't an impressive time anymore. But I have been a winner, a top finisher, always in the top ten, without going faster than nine days, twelve hours. But I won with nine days, seven hours and that was a slow win. So much is determined by the elements. But now everybody seems to beat the elements. The top twenty finishes are within ten days, whereas before you had a couple of teams maybe within ten days and the people who were brave and sneaked out in the storm. Well, now everybody's going. The winning time hasn't been dramatically improved, but definitely the top pack is all compressed. It's more competitive than ever. More people can do it.

When I won the first time in 2004, the thing that I remembered is that I had always dreamed of winning the Iditarod, my whole life since I was a kid. I had been thinking, *Someday I'm going to win the Iditarod* and imagining myself doing it. Suddenly, it was coming true. There I was mushing from Safety to Nome, the last twenty-two miles, in a good position, and nobody was going to catch me. I just sat back and relaxed the last part of that run, enjoyed it.

My whole life I had been waiting for that and now it was actually happening. I could hardly believe it. It was like one of those pinch-yourself moments. That's what I remember best. It was a validation. That was my eleventh try. Paul Harvey, the radio commentator, who always talked about "the rest of the story" said, "This year's Iditarod was won by a ten-time loser." I thought that was pretty good.

When I finished on Front Street and was under the burled arch I was kind of bewildered and confused. I was thinking, *Boy*, and grabbing at stuff. I remember the crowd was so receptive that I kind of went off and started shaking people's hands along the chute and Mark Nordman, the race marshal, had to come and grab me by the collar and get me back up there for TV and everything we were supposed to do. The second time was a little bit different because they actually planned for me to go around and shake hands for a few minutes. People come out to see you in the chute and you get hustled into the chute and they can't even see you from the sidelines.

In 2004 early on the race was really cold and I was able to lie back and take it easy and still enjoy a good, hard trail without it getting destroyed by a lot of teams ahead of me. I did some things strategically, almost by accident. Everybody's gotten a lot smarter about preserving a team. I shouldn't say everybody. We've seen some examples recently of not-so-much. Going out conservatively and hopefully being stronger at the end is the simple explanation.

On the run from Ophir to Cripple I remember the dogs just being phenomenal. They knocked that out even though it was warm weather and I remember feeling at that point it was a transitional run. I was toward the front at that point anyway. Different people take their mandatory twenty-four-hour rest in different places, so it turned out I was six hours behind leaving there. It took me until we went through Kaltag to actually regain the lead. I got to Unalakleet one minute behind the leader. It was Kjetil Backen from Norway.

Properly cared for and properly rested the dog team was really strong on those long, difficult runs. I've made too many mistakes between that year and this year and that's one of those things that should have been cemented in my memory from the lessons of the first win.

The weather was warmer in my second win, but we have to be the masters of our environment. So you can expect warm weather or cold weather, dry weather or deep snow, and we have to master all of that. There are teams that run a certain set schedule every time and when the year coincides with their style they do well, but the rest of the time, they don't. I think our dogs are capable of being more versatile than that. I hope to be able to react to different situations and do better. I think that's what we're starting to get a better handle on.

In 2013, the temperatures were really warm for the Iditarod. It rained hard on us on the Yukon River. I'd been carrying this set of rain gear with me for years, ever since I got rained on in 2005, and it was always in my sled and I never used it.

I finally used it in 2013 and I was the only one with a smile on my face at Shageluk and Grayling. Everybody else was cutting up trash bags and I was wearing this nice, green rain gear. I was wanting people to see me and take my picture. I was pretty happy with that. It was a big mental boost. Nobody was going to freeze to death out there, but you're miserable when you're soaking wet. It helped my mind-set, if nothing else. It was rainy and warm on the trail and there again I think our team was able to rise to the occasion as long as we gave them the right tools to work with—proper feeding, proper rest—for the conditions. I was really happy with how that went.

Some of the other mushers were coming back to me. The real question was who was winning the race all along. Sometimes some of the pundits like to think that people are lying back and are not going to win unless the front guy falters, but the fact is that the front guy was never winning in the first place. He was overrunning his team. He was not in position. He wasn't resting enough. The guy who ultimately wins is the only one who was in the right place at the right time. Sometimes they come from behind.

They're ahead physically, but one of the challenges of reporting and covering the race, and understanding the race, to my way of thinking (and I think Dallas would say the same thing) is that the most important statistic is invisible. It's the energy still in your dog team. It doesn't show up in the numbers.

I might be ahead or behind. I may have a faster trip or not. You can't quantify what's in the dogs. What I tried to do in 2013 was by the end of the race have a dog team that could not be passed. If I have a dog team that can't be passed, I'm going to have the best last run. Now you have to be in position. You can't be forever back there. Dallas had the fastest team on the last part of the race, but he was too far back because of problems and issues he had during the middle of the race. But he did a phenomenal job of just getting near the front. The reason he was able to pass people was because of what he built into his team. The team that had the fastest run is somewhat of an indication of who has the strongest team, but it might be the team that didn't flame out. So there is a control factor. There's only a certain amount you can see from the numbers.

In 2013 people were expecting me to get passed and beat at the end of the race because Aliy Zirkle had run faster than me from Elim to White Mountain by a half hour or so. It was a foregone conclusion among pundits that I was done. My view was that I had spent less energy getting there so now let's race. It worked out. Does that mean it will automatically work out next time? Absolutely not. This time it did. That's the way my team and her team were. She made a valiant effort and fell a little bit short. I felt as if I had preserved my team and it had energy at the end.

It took me ten years to get back to the finish line first. There was nothing foregone about any of it. When I left White Mountain with seventy-seven miles to go, most people except probably me, thought I was going to get passed. I took it easy until I got through the foothills and down to the beach again and when I finished snacking my dogs and ran across the big lagoon outside Nome, I looked back and there was my competition within sight, a half mile behind me.

Then it was time to start up. I thought, *Now is our chance. This is what we've been saving up for.* And we gained back twenty minutes. We were twenty-four minutes ahead of Aliy at Safety, something like that. We gained that time in a short shot. When you get to Safety you can see back far enough to see that nobody's there and certainly when you get to Cape Nome you can look back and see nobody's there. It was daytime, so I had good visibility and I felt really comfortable when I topped Cape Nome that unless we had some type of calamity that we should win. So that was a really fun ride from Cape Nome into Nome. The last eleven miles or so.

It was different from winning the first time. When I won the first time in 2004 I was in the category of young guys and the second time I guess they're saying I'm in the category of old guys. I still feel the same. But I had had some unpleasantries in the media. I'd been written off, thought some unnecessary personal things were said. So it was very satisfying to not be a has-been, not be done and not go off into the sunset, but to win another Iditarod. It validates the next decade of my racing. It's pretty clear to me now that the Iditarod is not just for younger guys. That's been the spin for a long time.

Look at Dallas Seavey and Pete Kaiser and Jake Berkowitz, but look at these older guys. All of a sudden, they realize we're actually the coaches, not so much the athletes and experience really does pay off. The record for the oldest musher winning the Iditarod has been broken many times. I think that like I said at the finish line as long as we're reasonably able to help our dogs up the hills and take good care of them in the checkpoints, there's no reason why you can't be well advanced in years and still be very competitive at this.

To be totally honest when Dallas won in 2012 there were mixed emotions. I was in the race trying to win. We had discussed how it would be cool if we came in one-two in any order. I think we would be equally happy with that. I was totally proud of Dallas for winning. I told him he did a good job. That's what I wanted for him. There's nothing better than for your son to grow up in your footsteps and even surpass you and do as well as he possibly can. But here we were trying to compete for the same goal and we both can't win. Now that I've won again, it sort of levels it out again, if you will. We're on equal footing and obviously if he keeps racing he's got more viable years ahead of him than I do. But I'm not sure that I may not still be racing after he's gone and doing something else.

Dallas and I have that understanding about being one-two. Dallas and I are best friends. It's beyond that. A lot of people are father and son. We've done a lot together with his wrestling. I was there with him through all of his wrestling exploits. I was at ringside when he won a national championship. I've been sort of coach and mentor. We've done all that together. He helped me as my main handler with the dogs when I won the first time in 2004. He was right there all the time. So we've been partners in a lot of things and if I'm not going to win, I sure hope he's winning.

We have been a mushing family since the first Iditarod, and Dad's always been my biggest believer in that I'm going to do well. That makes you feel good. In terms of public relations or family notoriety, that's been a blessing and a curse to some extent, but I like it for the most part. It's a good thing.

I guess I've never really thought of it in the collective. People say the Seaveys are mushing royalty or a dynasty, that kind of thing, but I always think of it individually. I just think it's been a really neat experience for us to share the race. My dad, me, three sons, and Conway will most likely do it, and Jen, my daughter-in-law, Dallas's wife. We have something in the family that we all like to talk about. Of course, after a while most of the women roll their eyes and go, "Guess what they're talking about?" I'm just really happy that I've had this as a backdrop to raising four boys and the experience with my dad has kept us together and communicating in a special way over the decades.

The Yukon River...
somewhere between Blackburn and
Kaltag...I sensed their presence in the
early morning light long before I saw
them. At first agitated, surprisingly
they soon settled down and became
spectators of our long journey.
An unforgettable feeling overcame
me as we passed beneath them ...
a special memory of my 1979 ...

IDITAROD

Early Morning Light, official Iditarod poster, 1989.

CHAPTER 5

Dick
MACKEY

orn in Concord, New Hampshire, in 1932, Dick Mackey never shed his New England accent although he has spent most of the rest of his adult life in Alaska since the 1950s. He got involved in dog mushing as a young man and first tested his dog driving skills in the Anchorage Fur Rendezvous sprint championships long before there was an Iditarod Trail Sled Dog Race.

Although his friend Dan Seavey remembers Mackey vacillating about whether or not to enter the first Iditarod in 1973, Mackey recalls things differently. He says that as soon as race founder Joe Redington Sr. told him about the idea he said, "I'll be the second to sign up." The reference was to his belief that Redington was going to be number one, although things didn't turn out that way.

Mackey did make the inaugural journey between Anchorage and Nome when mushers were feeling their way along the trail. In his dramatic style of storytelling, Mackey talks of women and children gathering around their menfolk at the starting line, giving them hugs and kisses as they disappeared one by one into the great unknown.

Mackey placed seventh in the first Iditarod and in 1978 he became an Iditarod champion when he captured the closest and tensest Iditarod, besting Rick Swenson by one second on the clock as the mushers ran down Front Street spurring their dog teams on.

Since the 1970s, the Mackeys have remained prominent in long-distance sled-dog racing. The next generation has exceeded Dick's popularity while sometimes matching and sometimes exceeding his accomplishments in the race. Son Rick won the 1983 championship. Another son, Bill, raced in 1984. Lance Mackey, a cancer survivor, electrified the mushing world with his achievements, winning the Iditarod four straight times in the 2000s. Son Jason has completed the race and still competes.

On another front, Dick Mackey once operated the farthest north truck stop in the world in remote Coldfoot, Alaska, and was on the premises when an all-time low temperature of eighty-two degrees below zero was recorded there as part of an extended cold snap. These days Mackey prefers to winter in Arizona, but he spends part of every year in Alaska, often during Iditarod time.

I was interested in an Iditarod race right from the beginning when I heard about it being planned. I was active in the sprint-mushing races, but there was a big difference between sprint races and long-distance races. The sprint races might have only been for ten miles in a day. I was keeping a bunch of dogs and running them ten miles on a Sunday afternoon. The idea of a long race meant there was a reason to work with them much more.

In 1966 Joe Redington and Dorothy Page had the idea for a race celebrating the centennial of the purchase of Alaska from Russia to be held in 1967. I went out and worked on clearing the trail over 9-Mile Hill out of Knik. When I was out there doing that, it just drove another nail in it for me, that I was hooked on mushing longer. Turned out longer was better.

For me the idea of a longer race meant there was more reason to have the dogs and work more with them in the wilderness. That was the fun part of it. The first year of the Iditarod in 1973 I wasn't that concerned about the racing part of it as much as enjoying being out there and just getting to Nome.

People forget how many doubters there were. A lot of people said we would never get to Nome and we really didn't know if we could or not. It sounded great, but it wasn't until we were two-thirds of the way up the trail that I even wondered how well I could do. Up until then I didn't care. It was just being out there, just the challenge of it. That was the idea of it.

Every one of us who were entered were outdoors people. We didn't know if we could do it or not, but we thought, *If anybody can do it, I can.* Contrary to today when you were mushing along you built a campfire and everybody camped around it and had a good time. Then the next morning you got up and you started out again. It was not set up to be that way with any kind of rules, since we were feeling our way, but back then it was a little bit like a stage race, like the Tour de France. You went as far as you could and stopped for the night. Now the race is so fast that mushers hardly stop at all when they don't have to and they don't camp with other competitors.

In 1987, the last time I ran the Iditarod, I was out on the trail between Iditarod and Shageluk. It was bitterly cold and I was not feeling that well. I had not been having good luck with the team and I stopped and built a fire. Well, along came son Rick. He said, "What are you doing, Dad?" I said, "I'm just taking a break and getting warm." He said, "I haven't seen a campfire in years."

Nobody wants to take the time to stop. Of course you wouldn't see one today either. Just because the race has changed doesn't mean that it's bad. It's just different because it is so much faster and every minute counts. But I don't think there is as much camaraderie as there was. There's no time. Nobody has time for that anymore.

Everybody has their own opinions about how things have changed. I hated to see the relationship change with the village checkpoints. It was a great thing when the mushers went to people's houses to eat dinner and spend the night. Once they went to corralling the mushers it changed the tone of it, but how do you keep it fair any other way? On the other hand, it's not fair anyway. One person operates on a shoestring and another person has got unlimited funds. That's not fair.

But it's still the adventure. As long as there are rookies coming in and there's a good attitude towards that, then it's OK. Let the pros fight it out and everybody else just try to make it under the arch.

It's a wonderful lure, just to get there. I told [musher] Cindy Abbott, "You have accomplished an awesome feat by climbing Mount Everest. But running the Iditarod, I think, is a greater feat, and I think you'll feel the same way." She got injured severely along the way and said she would be back to try again and I read that she said, "The Iditarod is far more difficult than climbing Mount Everest." To me, that's a hell of a statement because I'm in awe of anyone that climbs Mount Everest. Of course, I'm eighty and I'm not going to do either one now.

Now I find out Mount Everest is easy. Uh, huh. The reason I go to Arizona for about four months every year is because I don't like the cold anymore. I never in my wildest dreams thought I'd ever reach that point, you know. But I get back to Alaska for the race every year, that's the thing.

It has been more than forty years straight where there has been a Mackey in the race. I'm proud of that. Between four sons they've all completed it and two of them have won it. I'm proud, not for the wins, though I have enjoyed them, but just for the fact that they've been in it, carrying on the tradition. Maybe someday there will come a year when there is no Mackey on the starting list, but my granddaughter Brenda [Rick's daughter] will do it and eventually I think Jason's son Patrick will. Brenda's serious and she has done the Yukon Quest. She was only eighteen years old when she did the Quest.

People do call me the family patriarch, but I'm practically the patriarch of the race. I think there are only two Iditarod finishers alive who are older than me now, Ron Aldrich and Howard Farley.

There are mushers who enter the Iditarod who don't have a competitive bone in their bodies. My son Bill was like that. He felt he had to race it because everyone in the family was doing well. He had to get a belt buckle. Every rookie that gets into the race has two goals: getting a patch that they can wear with pride and a belt buckle. They want to get to Nome. They want to get to the finish line.

Completing the Iditarod, I can't think of another event in your life that will stay with you as much as that. It used to be that way for running a marathon, and maybe climbing a mountain. When you complete a marathon or climb a mountain, it's you against yourself. When you complete the Iditarod, it's you and a team of dogs. That's the kicker right there. That adds a whole different element.

Every competitive sport you're in, any undertaking that you have to condition yourself physically, mentally, whatever, what's the largest thing going, a football team? But you take sixteen dogs, you've got to speak their language, too, and they've got to understand yours and then you become a team together. That's difficult.

The 1978 race will always be special. Rick Swenson and I have always appreciated and admired each other. When Rick first started running [1976], even back then, I was one of the old men of the Iditarod. I appreciated him for being a young, big, rugged, tough-minded guy. Winning the race by one second is something that people never forget. It comes up so frequently. It isn't that Swenson won the race five times. I won just that once. It could have faded into the woodwork, but it didn't because it was a one-second finish.

Having that win entered into the Alaska Sports Hall of Fame as a special moment was the icing on the cake of my dog-mushing career. And having son Lance chosen as a member of the same class was equally important. That was a big deal. That really summed it up, not because it was Lance, it could have been any one of the boys. The fact that you're in the same class as any one of your kids was a big deal.

That moment was entered into the Alaska Sports Hall of Fame, not because I beat Rick Swenson or that I won since I only won once, but because of the degree of the win. They haven't had a race like it since.

One of the great things about having my sons racing is that I can still watch the Iditarod with a rooting interest and I don't have to get out there and get cold. You stop and think and since right after the first race in 1973, the Iditarod has been the biggest part of my life. You have your employment and you raise your kids, but the Iditarod has been the biggest factor in my life. And forty years have passed! Whew!

Of course the race has changed. Everything changes. When I first came to Anchorage there were about five paved streets. Now it has about three hundred thousand people. I always tell people that I used to train my dogs where the Northway Mall is now. In 1969 I had a chance to buy a 160-acre homestead for $15,000. But who the hell had $15,000 when you're making $4.50 or $5.00 an hour and raising a family? I moved out to the Mat-Su Valley in 1970.

From its beginnings the Iditarod has become the biggest sporting event in Alaska, which brings out the most passion. It is the biggest sporting event in the world in dog mushing. The Iditarod is what makes people aware of other dog-mushing events.

In Alaska, it's something that people care about whether or not they are really sports fans. It's the one thing on the calendar. Everyone knows about the Iditarod. They may not know the details and they may not follow it on a day-to-day basis, but they certainly follow it on an annual basis.

CHAPTER 6

Jason
MACKEY

*P*art of the second generation of Mackey Iditarod racers, Jason Mackey chased his third Iditarod finish in the 2014 race. In a recent rarity his brother Lance, a four-time champion, was not entered, taking a break from the one-thousand-mile event, and Jason was able to combine forces with dogs from his own kennel and his pick of those from Lance's kennel.

Jason Mackey, forty-two, was born in Alaska and spent his youth split between the Matanuska-Susitna Valley after his father, Dick, moved his dog operations fifty miles from Anchorage, and then in the remote area of Coldfoot during the time period when his dad ran the truck stop for vehicles bringing shipments into and out of the oil fields at Deadhorse on Prudhoe Bay.

The younger Mackey likes to say that he has been around sled dogs since he was born and given that the family always had huskies, it is an accurate assessment. As a teenager he competed in the Junior Iditarod four times and in the Junior World Championship sprint-mushing race in Anchorage four times, as well. When Jason Mackey says it is his goal to become the next Mackey Iditarod champion there is no reason to doubt him and every reason to believe that it is possible. He would be following in the footsteps of father Dick (one title), brother Rick (one title), and brother Lance (four titles).

Professionally, Jason works as a heavy equipment operator. He and his wife, Lisa, have two sons. Similar to the outdoors interests of the other males in his family, Jason enjoys hunting, fishing, and backcountry hiking.

Mackey made his Iditarod debut in 2004 and as a rookie placed twenty-sixth in the field, winning $3,300. In 2008, Mackey returned and finished in thirty-third place, winning $1,049. They were paydays, but also illustrate how difficult it can be for long-distance mushers to make money from their passion. Mackey had some bad luck during the 2013 race and was forced to scratch partway to Nome. He has also competed in the Yukon Quest, the one-thousand-mile race between Whitehorse, Yukon Territory, and Fairbanks, Alaska.

Hoping to make his mark in the Iditarod as so many members of his family have done, Jason Mackey maintains a sense of humor about growing up in a mushing family.

It wasn't a law that I had to become a musher, but it was what we knew, and I was always around it. Sometimes I've said, "Why couldn't we have raced cars or something? Why did it have to be dogs?" I love my life and I love dogs, but it keeps you broke. You get sucked into it. Of course, whether it be race cars, sailboats, or dogs, it's expensive and you put 100 percent into it.

It doesn't matter what it takes to do it, I'm going to do it. It may be a hobby for some mushers. Some people say, "I want to race the Iditarod." Or they say, "I want to race dogs." They do it for a little while and they get out. I have no intention of ever getting out of dogs.

I'm in my forties now and I've been doing this since I was big enough to hang on to a sled. My dad tells stories of Lance and me in the dog lot carrying little pails that you take to the beach, little kids' pails, and a shovel and feeding the dogs and cleaning up after them. We were living in Wasilla and after moving around I'm back there on the same property that I was raised on

This is where the family moved when it was no longer possible to have a dog team in Anchorage. The family lived in South Anchorage, but it's all developed. There is absolutely no way you could have a dog team there. They used to run dogs right down the street that now would have bumper-to-bumper traffic.

It's almost impossible to run dogs where I live in Wasilla, too. I have had to truck dogs to trails, back and forth. So for the 2014 race I made up my mind that I was not going to truck dogs. I was going to build a camp at Port McKenzie or on the Denali Highway, near Denali National Park. As long as there is snow and I'm near a river. Then I planned to spend time with my brother Rick in Nenana training.

Training has become so expensive between fuel and dog food, so it's better to be stationed in one spot at a time. It's kind of hard to go look for another piece of property, too. When I moved off the Kenai Peninsula, I couldn't really find a spot where I wanted to be. When my parents divorced my mom got a ten-acre piece of property on Pitman Road. It's road accessible. I've got to go to work. I can't move into the Bush and make a living. You can't make a living at what we do with dogs. You have to have a job. My mother offered it and I took her up on it. I said, "OK, I'll build a house on the end of your stretch." She gave me two and a half acres, but people don't like it that I have fifty or sixty dogs there. I'm about three or four miles from Iditarod Trail headquarters.

It's a ten-acre property, and there are two other properties fairly close. One is a former sprint musher and his wife and they don't mind the dogs. Another was owned by a former dog musher, but now there is a wrecking yard. I can hear the cars banging around there, but I don't complain about it. But they do complain about the dogs.

When I moved the dogs in there they asked, "Are they going to bark?" I said, "Haven't you ever heard a dog bark?" You might say I was kind of stubborn about it. My family has been there for about forty years, regardless of whether or not I was on that property. My mom's still there. Basically, we're grandfathered in. I had a little dispute with the Humane Society. They asked how many dogs I was going to have. I said, "I'm gonna have as many dogs as I want to put on the property."

Lavon Barve [former Iditarod contender] is right up the street. Some of the people that lived there years ago still live there now, but without dogs. They don't like to see that junkyard that used to be a dog lot. Lavon's even stopped by my house many times and said, "Hey, it's really cool to see you still have dogs around here."

We reviewed the trail system and he told me how he used to run out of his place in the late 1990s. Now you have to have some crossing guards or you're going to get run over. People don't look for us with dog teams anymore. It's no different in Knik. Ray Redington Jr., in the capital of the mushing world, got hit twice. People just don't know. They're not aware. They move out to the Matanuska-Susitna Valley from different places and they have to know that this is what we do. Everybody's on snowmachines going ninety miles per hour. We have to watch out for them. You don't just pull out into a street without looking to see if something is coming. We do everything and anything to make sure that the dogs are safe, but people don't think of dog teams. That's one reason I was leaving good training grounds around home to make a camp.

It does mean the world to me to be part of the Mackey mushing family and that we have such a long tradition and connection to the Iditarod, even if I do joke about it and say that about why couldn't Dad have been a car racer. My niece, Brenda, Rick's daughter, is going to be the next up-and-coming Mackey to race. She's been doing some middle-distance racing with her eye on the Iditarod one year. Her daughter Isabel just won a one-dog class race.

Isabel is just as doggy as Brenda is. So it keeps going. The Mackey family, the Seavey family, the Redington family, we're all the same. We don't want to see it die. My wife and I have two boys, Patrick, twenty-one, and Jason, nineteen. My nineteen-year-old isn't so much into racing, but he loves the dogs. Patrick works on the Mendenhall Glacier in Juneau giving rides to tourists with Linwood Fiedler. He's got his eye on qualifying for the Iditarod and running it in 2015. I couldn't be more proud of them, but I've warned them about being sucked in. He says, "You can warn me all you want."

Patrick is really passionate about what he does. I enjoyed my upbringing and his is like mine. It made me a good person, hardworking, responsible, spending the time with the dogs. You can't just up and leave and go on vacation. You can't just say, "Well, I'm going to Hawaii for two weeks." I can't ask somebody to take care of my fifty dogs while I take off and go on vacation. So the boys know they're getting sucked into this vortex of a dog life and they've been warned. That's all I can say. I did my part.

At the same time I'm glad that one of the two boys, Patrick really, is no different than Lance or Rick or myself. He wants to win. I've always told them being part of the Iditarod is not about winning. I talked to my dad and I told him that I want to win the Iditarod and that's why I keep doing this. I had a bad year in 2013 and I had a bad Quest in 2009. But we're not a family that just throws in the towel and gives in. You've got to put your head down and keep going.

My first Iditarod in 2004 was probably when I had the most fun on the trail. It was my rookie year. It wasn't Lance's rookie year, but he had a tough year and as it worked out he was farther back than he wanted to be. We ran together on the trail almost all of the way from Anchorage to Nome. It was a fun time. It was an emotional time. When I look back on that race I think, *What a great time.* There's one thing in life that I'll never forget and that's my first Iditarod. Lance finished twenty-fourth and I finished twenty-sixth.

One of the highlights of my rookie Iditarod occurred when we got ready to leave White Mountain, seventy-seven miles from Nome. The people who were mushing the Serum Run reenactment had left that morning. One of the trail-breakers came back to White Mountain on a snowmachine and told us about the trail ahead: "It's impassable. It's blowing sixty miles per hour and there are drifts four feet high. You can't get through." Lance and I looked at each other and said, "We're seventy miles from Nome, man. We're going to Nome."

It was quite the journey. At one moment I questioned why the hell we were so stubborn because it was really blowing. I didn't know up from down. The only time I could see my leader was when she was standing next to me. She turned around at one point and I became the lead dog. But it really was only for a short time and then it cleared up.

When we left it was daylight and we mushed into the dark and by the time we got to the blow hole out there it was black. I had never been there before and it was night and blowing hard and I really couldn't tell north from south. It was just like all of the stories I had heard over the years. There's a stretch where it blows off the Bering Sea when I ain't never seen anything like it. When you get through it you're like, *If I can get through that there's nothing on earth that I can't do.*

My second Iditarod was just a blur by comparison. In 2013 I entered the race and I was going along and got into waist-deep water. There were some holes where there was water where it was just ridiculous because the temperature was too warm. It was just another hurdle. It's what we do. You get through the water and get to the other side and you dry out. It was forty degrees. It was just horrible. Everything was just saturated, but I didn't build a fire. I ended up scratching more than eight days into the race.

On the Iditarod it's going to be forty below and forty above. It may be snowing, it may be calm. Sometimes it's going to be raining. Getting ready for my fourth Iditarod I know I haven't seen what Martin Buser and DeeDee Jonrowe and Jeff King have seen over the years, but I'm pretty sure I've seen all of the conditions. I've seen sixty below and it was fifty-two above in Cripple. We were sitting in Cripple on a break looking at the thermometer. Nobody was moving because it was too hot for the dogs. Fifty-two above? You've got to be kidding me. This is the Iditarod?

So I have seen it from one extreme element to the next, even the sun tanning element. We trained in Coldfoot for years when my dad had the Coldfoot truck stop. So I was used to fifty below from that. That gets your attention. You had best know what you're doing when it's that cold out. You get into a situation with the temperature like that and you'd better have all the good equipment to be prepared to live. My older brother Bill, who lived in Bettles then, taught me a lot of survival skills from experience in the Brooks Range. If you don't know survival skills you're not going to survive. I don't care if it's summer or winter.

In Coldfoot in the winter months, forty-five below zero was a normal day. The thermometer would plunge to sixty-five below and we'd still be out breaking trail with the dogs. Most people say, "After forty below it's all the same." Wrong. That is absolutely false. I can handle forty below, and most people can. When it hits sixty-five or seventy below, things are different. I've dealt with keeping dogs alive. At those temperatures, things break. They do and you don't even have to touch them. When it's that cold, if you drop something it shatters. It shatters like glass. I've heard people say that if you take a glass of water out at fifty below that it vaporizes in the air. It doesn't at fifty below, but it does at sixty-five below.

People may think it's a myth, but I actually experienced it. I'm not saying I enjoy sixty below. Don't get me wrong because there's nothing to enjoy about it other than you can say, "I made it through," so then you can talk about it.

In 2013 I had a team that for the first half of the race, until I got sick, that I really thought I had a race going. I was right up near the top with every-body. You learn something new every year. Every time you pull the hook you learn something. Years and years of doing this, and I don't care who you ask, every run is different. You always learn something. My goal in 2014 was to stay healthy and that the dogs would stay healthy.

Lance was taking time off from the race and I got to add to my dogs from some of his. I want to win the Iditarod. I don't want to be sixty years old and still trying to win it. Lance, Rick, and Dad all won on their sixth attempt. The 2014 race was my fourth attempt.

I didn't have the best record in the Iditarod, but I know what I'm doing. I have a whole bunch of knowledge with me since I have three of the best mushers in the world teaching me. We put all of our heads together and got input on all kinds of strategies. They've proven that they are winners and it's time for me to prove myself as a winner.

Racing the Iditarod is not just the dogs. It's not just the musher. It's a combination and a whole bunch of luck. No matter how many times you run it, no matter how many times you prepare for it, putting together the food in drop bags for the checkpoints, it's a different adventure. You have a plan. You know what you want to do. But it's still an adventure.

Flying High, limited edition print, 2003.

CHAPTER 7

Lance
MACKEY

espite owning the last name Mackey and being part of one of the Alaska clans with the longest ties to the Iditarod Trail Sled Dog Race, no one saw Lance Mackey coming. One minute he was just a guy who had competed in the Iditarod like so many others and the next minute he was unbeatable.

From also-ran to champion seemed like an overnight journey for Mackey as he accomplished unprecedented feats in long-distance mushing. Until Mackey did it, no one believed that it was possible to win the one-thousand-mile Yukon Quest and the one-thousand-mile Iditarod in one season. The effort was felt to be too tiring for the dogs—and probably the musher, too. Instead, Mackey showed the back-to-back races were probably beneficial for a top racing team.

Mackey won the Yukon Quest four years in a row between 2005 and 2008 and he became the only musher to win the Iditarod four years in a row between 2007 and 2010. His fourth Iditarod triumph was one of only a few sub-nine-day championship races. Mackey's accomplishments were all recorded following a life-threatening bout with throat cancer. Mackey's dog operation is appropriately named "Comeback Kennel." After his multiple victories in the challenging Quest and Iditarod some referred to Mackey as "the world's toughest athlete." For sure he was one of the most inspirational ones.

Cancer treatments alone sapped his strength, ruined his taste buds, and made it difficult for him to remain hydrated. Some side effects continue to bother Mackey today at age forty-four and resulted in him taking a leave of absence from competition in both the Quest and Iditarod. In early 2014 it was revealed that aftereffects from his cancer treatment were resulting in his losing his teeth and that his medical insurance did not cover his bills. Donations were solicited to help Mackey cope with the costs of his problems.

In-between his illness and the unfortunate turn Mackey experienced, however, the Fairbanks dog driver's achievements electrified mushing fans and led to his being inducted into the Alaska Sports Hall of Fame. He also shifted his attention to sprint racing and entered the Anchorage Fur Rendezvous World Championship in 2014, one of the events where his father, Dick, got his start racing decades earlier. Mackey wrote a book about his life and a forthcoming documentary was expected.

Although Mackey did not enter long-distance races until he was in his thirties, growing up in the dog-oriented Mackey family he said he always thought he would try them. Before he won any long-distance race, the Quest or Iditarod, Mackey endured considerable adversity, from spending years finding his vocation and overcoming a battle with drugs, to his highly publicized fight with cancer.

I tell people I've been in mushing since I was in the womb. I was forced into it. My mother, Kathi Smith, was racing when she was seven months pregnant with me. It's true.

After that I was handling dogs since I was old enough to mush. I was scooping out dog food for my father's dogs when we lived in Wasilla from the time I was three or four years old and I raced in the one-dog class at Tudor Track in Anchorage when I was five. Between ages fourteen and seventeen I entered the Junior Iditarod. But there weren't a lot of kids' races and at that point I stopped, from about age seventeen to twenty-nine. I took a little break.

For a while I was a Bering Sea fisherman and during the Iditarod I would always listen to the race on the radio from the wheelhouse. People were always asking me when I was going to do it and I didn't have an answer.

I didn't want to make a commitment. I was making good money fishing and I didn't want to spend it on dogs.

Then I moved to the Kenai Peninsula. I was married with kids and I lived right around the corner from Tim Osmar, who was racing the Iditarod. We had eight or nine dogs and the kids, Amanda and Britain, liked them. I wanted them to learn responsibility and they liked riding with the dogs on the beach down there. Having dogs had nothing to do with me wanting to do the Iditarod.

But next thing I knew I was going to the Soldotna sprint-mushing track and getting to be friends with other mushers. It was starting to rekindle my original interest in dogs from when I was a kid. It was just an easy fit. I bought a sled for $200 and collected some free dogs. By then it was not just the kids and the dogs, I wanted to do it, too.

Within a year, by 1999, we had twenty dogs. It was just living in the neighborhood with other dog mushers that rubbed off on me. I started doing well in the short races. These were ten-milers. But invariably I would get the last paying position. Remember, these were all dogs that nobody else wanted because they didn't think they were fast enough. I wasn't raising dogs or breeding dogs. I just did a little training with them. I started to think, *What if I put a little effort into this?*

I didn't have many dogs or much money, but I decided, *I'm gonna run the Iditarod next year.* That was 2001. I was just like any other Alaskan who wanted to do the race. I was going to do it once. That was it. I did the Copper Basin 300 as my first qualifying race. Then I did the Clam Gulch Classic for my second one. I won that one.

So I entered the Iditarod in 2001. My rookie race I finished thirty-sixth out of fifty-seven finishers. My thinking was that I was going on a leisurely camping trip to get a finisher's belt buckle. My thoughts were that *I'm never going to do this again, so maybe I can have some fun and make some memories.* Some people said, "I told you so" that I wasn't really ready. But all it did was motivate me more. I started thinking that thirty-sixth wasn't bad and *What if I do this and this?* I could finish much better. It wasn't a realistic daydream at the time. I put everything I owned financially into doing the first one and I won $1,049.

Before long I was dealing with something much bigger than the Iditarod, cancer stuff. When I went into the hospital after the race I didn't know whether I was going to live or die. I entered in 2002, but that race I was sick and I didn't finish. I did win the Most Inspirational Musher Award. I did that race with a feeding tube in me. When I was at my sickest, thinking of doing the Iditarod again was one of those things that I could look forward to in order to keep me going. Me doing the Iditarod was something that made my parents proud and it was an opportunity for me to change my life. It was just a familiar family dream.

Everybody tried to talk me out of starting the 2002 Iditarod. I wasn't very strong. But I learned something about myself. I was pretty stubborn. It wouldn't have looked good if I had gone out there and passed away on the Iditarod. I pulled out in Ophir. I felt like a complete loser. I had had so much support. I felt like I was letting down so many people, friends, supporters, doctors. I had huge doubt. I sat there at the checkpoint for about two days before I decided I wasn't going to make it to the finish. In the end I gave Bill Borden, who was from Georgia, my sled. He finished fifty-third.

After that I worked on rebuilding my health. I didn't enter the Iditarod in 2003. I just did middle-distance races. I needed to get my health up to par. In 2004 I entered the Iditarod and my brother Jason and I ran together and took twenty-fourth and twenty-sixth. I was just trying to get better physically and get better as a dog musher.

Hugh Neff was the one who said to me, "You should come and do the other one-thousand-mile race." So in 2005 I entered the Yukon Quest and I won the Quest as a rookie. That just shot everything right up in my thinking. That just built up my confidence in a huge way. I took that same dog team and brought it to the Iditarod and I finished seventh. At that time it was still considered radical to be able to race the same dogs in the Quest and the Iditarod in the same year. But that was the beginning of changing the thinking. In a sense I came out of nowhere when I won the Quest and finished seventh in the Iditarod that year.

After that I won four Quests in a row and four Iditarods in a row. It is crazy. No one in the world, including my family and fans would ever have really thought I could do that. It blows my mind sometimes when I think of it. I think of myself as a musher who is not done yet, as someone who has really just started. There are eighty more things for me to learn. Winning those races four times in a row is a fantasy becoming a reality. That's exactly what it was.

The Iditarod has become so competitive, with so many good mushers who have a chance to win, I still don't know how I won four times in a row. When I was closing in on winning the first one in 2007, when it started becoming a reality, when it looked like I had a chance, I remember going down the trail on the back of the sled with a big grin on my face. And then when I got a little bit closer to Nome, I just started crying. It was such an emotional high.

I didn't really think I was going to win that Iditarod until I got to Cape Nome, outside of the city of Nome. I got down on my knees out there and I hugged every one of the dogs. I was laughing and crying. I was with one of my leaders, Larry, and I pointed down the trail to Nome and I said, "I know you know where we're at. But we're here first this time." Larry looked over at me and he kind of smiled and I swear he winked at me, as if he was saying, *I know, Dad.* My dogs knew I was going to win the Iditarod. As we came down Front Street Larry was in lead and he just strutted, his chest out.

Finishing that Iditarod in first place was one of the greatest moments of my life. It was louder than most moments in my life with the spectators lining the fencing on both sides of the street. My parents were there at the finish and they were crying for me. To be honest, for a long time I did a lot of things they weren't really proud of [Mackey has publicly detailed some of his drug problems when he was younger] and they were really proud of me that day. That was probably better than winning the Iditarod. I hugged my mom. My thinking was, *Dreams do come true.*

After I won those races one of the neatest things that happened was being voted into the Alaska Sports Hall of Fame and being inducted at the same time as my dad for his 1978 race against Rick Swenson. In a million years I never thought it would happen that I would be in the Alaska Sports Hall of Fame. It was pretty amazing to be recognized by the people like that. I was thinking, *I'm just some guy from Alaska who runs dogs.* It was, *Really? Me?* And again I was thinking that I was pretty young in the sport and that I've really just gotten started in the Iditarod.

That's one of my most recognized trophies in the house. That's mind-boggling to me.

CHAPTER 8

Joe MAY

A musher from another generation, Joe May, seventy-eight, of Trapper Creek, Alaska, owns the distinction of winning the 1980 Iditarod. He made his debut in the race in 1976 with an eleventh-place finish, finished fifth in 1979, became champion in 1980, and raced once more, in 1982, when he was honored with the Humanitarian Award.

May, whose son Mark also became a long-distance musher, won the 1980 race by thirteen hours over the revered Herbie Nayokpuk of Shish-maref. He also edged out such up-and-coming stars as Rick Swenson and Susan Butcher.

Originally from Sturgeon Bay, Wisconsin, May spent two decades working on freighters with a master's license on the Great Lakes. One of the requirements of the job was that he pass a physical exam each year and when he was thirty-seven years old he flunked it because of a medical problem. May's license expired and he had to find a new career. He hoped to work in Canada, but on a trip west and north he found himself in Haines in 1972 and instead settled in Alaska.

May benefited from a homesteading program that allowed him to claim a five-acre plot of land. Partially because of poor health he did not want to work right away and the idea of spending a couple of years on his own land, carving out a new niche in life in Alaska had great appeal for him.

Those circumstances led to May to becoming a permanent Alaska resident, taking up dog mushing, and becoming an Iditarod champion.

After I ran into my health problem, in a matter of weeks my license was gone and I put everything I wanted to keep in the backseat of a Fiat convertible and headed to Seattle. I went to Seattle to try to sort out my life and get it back together. Looking into a trip into Canada I ended up in Haines in Southeast Alaska. I picked up a hitchhiker who told me about this land program and I thought if I could find a place to build a cabin, a nice quiet place to read for a couple of years, that was all I wanted out of life.

I was really sick. I was in bad shape. I found the land. I built the cabin. But I also realized you really have to work here in Alaska. It was chopping wood and hauling water and stuff like that. I'd come off of ships where I had a cigarette burning at each end of the pilothouse and a cup of coffee in each hand. I worked six hours on and six hours off for seven days a week for months and months. It just destroys you. I got myself healthy and I did an entire turnaround. A neighbor gave me a dog and one dog started the whole thing of me mushing.

The nearest neighbor was a mile or a mile and a half away. There was no road, but there was a trail and it was fourteen miles to the mailbox. There was no post office or building here and my neighbor would hook up two or three dogs to his bicycle and in the summer that's how he would get his mail. It was twenty-eight miles round-trip and every time they'd cross the creek the dogs would get a drink, lay in the creek for a little while, and cool off. It looked like so much fun that after a while everyone in the area was using dogs in front of bicycles. I had one dog and I had to get another dog and three dogs was really good. It was hard on the bicycles, but it was really fun. I had already been running a trapline using snowshoes.

I had been trapping for marten, so of course once I had three dogs I made a little homemade sled and started with dogs from there. My sons, Mark and Paul, who were finishing high school in Michigan, came up. That's when it became sled dogs. We had a half-dozen dogs and we had to get a few more and add another one here and there. My trapline expanded. It got to where I was running a hundred miles of traplines and the boys were with me.

So it evolved like it did for a lot of mushers back then. You didn't ever intend to be a dog musher, but you just got to be one because of circumstances.

In 1975, Dick Mackey, Joe Redington, and Ron Aldrich came to visit and said they wanted to run a three-hundred-mile race around here. I didn't know anything about the Iditarod. Just the word, the name, that's all. They wanted to run a preliminary race through this country and they were looking for a trail. They knew that Harry Sutherland [later a six-time Iditarod racer] and I were trapping here and they wanted to know if they could use our trail system. We said, "Sure."

They held a meeting at the old Montana Creek Lodge that's gone now and Harry and I went to show them on the map where the trail went. Dick said, "Why don't you guys come along on the race?" I think Harry had seven or eight dogs and I had maybe ten or eleven. They weren't racing dogs. They were all different sizes, but they were good, tough dogs, trapping dogs. They were tough and slow.

I said, "I don't know. We don't have the equipment. We've never raced." Dick said, "Come along. It'll be fun. You can camp with a nice bunch of guys." So Harry said, "Sure, why not?" We had homemade trapping sleds and little flashlights. The harnesses were homemade. Half of our tools were homemade. We cooked over wood-made fires, no Coleman stoves. I won this new race, though Harry didn't finish.

I thought I was doing everything wrong. I felt I really shouldn't be where I was. It was my first race and at the end of the first day I was running two hours ahead of everybody. I was panicked because Mackey had said in Skwentna that I had ruined the dog team. I said, "How the hell could I have ruined them? They're only doing what they want to do."

It took Harry and I a day to figure things out and then we figured the other guys were really naïve. They seemed to believe anything anybody told them. We had a great time out there, but Harry scratched twenty-five miles from the finish. He was upset, but he had a really tired dog and he didn't want to jeopardize this dog. The race finished in Talkeetna and I think I won by six hours.

After the race Harry and I had a meeting over a bottle of wine. Trapping was balled up. We weren't ever gonna trap again if we didn't have to. Here we were running these ragtag, homemade outfits and there was money out there in mushing. We came to the realization that the grounding we had on the trapline, where there was no schedule, where the trail was rotten, and the dogs ate and drank when they could meant they had to be tough. The other guys training for the race were on a schedule. The dogs went home to a warm house every night and a warm bowl of food. That's what they were accustomed to. Dogs are creatures of habit. We weren't creatures of habit, nor were our dogs. It was to our advantage. So we decided, yeah, we're gonna do the Iditarod. I think that was December of 1975.

Harry was a poster boy for poverty dog driving. His total food for the 1976 Iditarod was a dead cow that some farmer had lost near the Matanuska-Susitna Valley. He chopped it up into twenty pieces and sent it out on the trail and that was his dog food. Alaska Sausage Company was his only sponsor and I think they gave him thirty-five linear feet of caribou sausage. I had a friend whose wife made up twenty hamburgers with no mustard, no ketchup, no onions, just a piece of meat between two buns, wrapped up in wax paper and frozen, plus Hershey bars. Each checkpoint I got one set of that. That was to keep me alive for three weeks. That's what we shipped out. I had some pretty decent dog food, fish. So Harry and I went out racing in the 1976 Iditarod. It didn't feel much different than the trapline.

In those days it was common in the race to team up with another musher. Harry and I traveled together and we cooked the caribou sausage on a pocketknife over a fire. One musher would cook the dog food and the other would cook the human food and you rotated. Sometimes in the villages someone would offer you a bowl of stew. In Ruby the guys running ahead of us had pretty much almost emptied the shelves in the store. The only thing left was a case of blueberry Pop Tarts. We bought the case. We did 75 or 150 miles of the Yukon River on frozen Pop Tarts exclusively.

We were running pretty far back at the time and we came upon two mushers together and they had a campfire going. It was Jerry Austin and Ford Reeves. Jerry goes, "Are you Sutherland and May?" Like we're a dance team or something. He said, "We heard we should keep an eye out for you guys because you were going to make a move up here on the Coast somewhere, that you're pretty tricky."

It didn't even really feel like a race compared to now. We went for days without seeing anybody. Harry didn't have many dogs. There was a homesteader on Petersville Road who had a big, shaggy, red dog and it was a car chaser. The only thing that dog named Clyde did was chase cars. Around ten days to two weeks before the Iditarod Harry went to the owner and asked him if he could borrow Clyde and give him a mushing audition. Harry put a harness on him and raced the dog in the team. The dog ran the Iditarod. Clyde was in the middle of the team going up Front Street and Harry finished third in the Iditarod.

For most of the race Harry and I ran together. In Koyuk we had a conference and Harry told me he didn't have enough money to get home from Nome if he didn't win some prize money. He was that far down on his cash. I at least had plane fare home. He said in Koyuk, "I'm going to take a chance. I'm going to go for it." I was afraid to do that because if my dog team crashed I wouldn't be able to get to the finish line. Harry went for it and I stayed behind. I rested more. Harry finished third and I finished eleventh.

That was the end of trapping for both of us for a while. We gradually changed dogs, but the advantage we had from trapping experiences served us well for two or three years. One reason was that at that time the Iditarod had bad trail or no trail a lot. The other guys training usually had nice trails. They had snowmachine preparation. Their dogs weren't accustomed to rough trail. Most of the other mushers snowshoed in front of their teams. On a trapline the dogs wouldn't know what to do if you did that. That was partly why the Native drivers had an advantage in the early years, too.

After I stayed home for a couple of years I started breeding faster dogs. I had helped develop some commercial dog food, too, with Alaska fish byproducts and Delta barley. I worked with someone and we were selling it commercially. It had been tested in races for two hundred or three hundred miles, but never at the stress level that you reach on the Iditarod. I got halfway into the 1979 race out of Ophir and the dogs had digestive upset problems from the dog food. There was nobody in sight behind me. The dogs got sick and I had to shut them down and switch dog food. It cost me a whole day. I had to wait until everybody caught up.

I had to have some salmon. The only thing that was going to straighten out my dogs' stomachs was dried fish. Jim Fleming, a trapper that I knew, lived there with his family. He was a hard-core trapper with his wife and kids. I asked him if he had some dried fish and he said, "We'll count." He had to feed his own dogs until the next season. He picked out about a dozen fish for me and said, "I can spare these." I said, "Let me give you some money." He said, "Oh, no. I can't take money for these because I caught these on a subsistence permit." There wasn't a game warden around for two hundred miles, Jim Fleming probably didn't have $50 to his name, and his knee was sticking through on his pants. That went beyond the meaning of integrity. The man was just that way. What was right was right and what was wrong was wrong. I got there before any of the other mushers and had dinner with him. He said in the spring, after the snow melted, he was going to move. He said, "I can't stay here. It's too crowded." Crowded? He said there were people living seven miles away, so he was being crowded out. He wouldn't tell me where he was going, but apparently it was a place where the closest neighbor was going to be more than seven miles away.

I should have won that race. I had the best team out there. I finished fifth because of sick dogs. I went home in 1979, fixed up my dog food, and went right back into training. We trained all though the summer. We never shut them down, so that team was in training for over two years. I lost a dog. I don't know when she died. She died in the dog lot from a liver problem. I had to look for a replacement and I didn't have a replacement that year to match that dog. A dog is a cog in a clock with a lot of cogs. If you put the wrong cog in there, it's not going to fit. I went to my friends and asked to borrow a dog, or lease a dog to try it out. I said, "I want the best one you've got." I went through I don't know how many dog yards and kept taking them back. That was a problem. How do you take a man's best dog back and say it's not good enough? You have to be really creative with alibis and reasons for returning it. It ended up being close to the race and I still had not found a replacement. I had a young dog in the yard. I think it was only eleven months old. I had been using it as a temporary fill-in, so it had miles on it. So I took him essentially for the lack of another dog to fill in with the team.

When I got into McGrath my girlfriend was there who had helped train the team—I wasn't married then—and when she asked how the dogs were doing I said, "There's nothing out here that can touch this dog team." She said, "You're drunk or smoking something." I said, "No, I've never driven anything like this team in my life." And I think Herbie Nayokpuk was thirty minutes ahead of me into McGrath. Herbie had a nice team. It was me and Herbie and Ernie Baumgartner into Ophir.

There was a prize for the halfway leader and Ernie woke me up and said, "Do you want to race?" Herbie was a man of a lot of integrity. We had a conference in the middle of the night about what to do and we all decided Herbie should go because he had led us into Ophir. We thought one of the three of us would win the race and if we raced for the halfway prize it might save the teams and we would all benefit. From then on we would come into a checkpoint and whoever was first left word with the checker to tell the other two guys what time they were leaving. We did it that way to give the dogs and ourselves adequate rest. We knew we would pick a spot farther down the line when we would all go racing to the end.

Herbie dropped back in Koyuk. He had sled trouble or dog trouble. At White Mountain, seventy-seven miles from the finish, the ham radio operator told me Herbie had called ahead to say that he was staying in Golovin so I could rest the dogs for a few hours longer and could get some sleep. There was that kind of integrity at the front. It was a gentleman's race. I tell that for the public. It seems there have been races where people are sneaking out on others and some sniping. It just never seemed to have very much class.

At times when I traveled near some of those top people they didn't know what I was going to do. It was none of their business. My thought was you make your own mistakes—that was bad enough—but if you're driving off of somebody else and watch what he's doing you're just adding his mistakes to your own. Until 1979 there was no schedule of run and rest. In the old system it was just run the dogs until they were tired and then sleep for a while and run them until they're tired again. Then it rolled into an hour thing, run six hours, rest six hours. It turned out the best schedule for the dogs turned out to be the best schedule for humans.

I was very happy when I got to Nome as the 1980 winner. I slept and ate ice cream. It sounds as if it was for celebration, but it was actually the best thing for caloric deficiency. I was interested in knowing how much weight you lose doing the race and my first race I lost thirteen pounds. I couldn't imagine it. I weighed one of my dogs, Angus, and Angus stayed exactly the same, not even a pound down.

The race changed in 1982. Money and other things began to affect it. It wasn't the same. I'm sure there are people who go out there and find the adventure on their first race in the Iditarod the way I did in my first race. You can still run into trees and the Dalzell Gorge is always different. It's magic for them. Some middle-aged lady from Florida comes to Alaska with a dream and leases a dog team and as long as she doesn't hurt the dogs, I think it will be something she'll never forget. It just wasn't like that for me anymore. That had all gone away.

Some mushers are still in it from when I raced. They turned it into a career, into a job. There were no professionals in the beginning. Everybody was a beginner. I could never get my mind around that there are still mushers doing the Iditarod after thirty years. We're all different people. Some people it's the only thing they've done and that's not to denigrate anyone. Cowboy Smith, way back, said to me one day, "Anyone who is going to run this thing more than three times and win it, they should buy a motorcycle." I think he meant to do something else if you can.

I pay attention to the Iditarod when it's going on, but I haven't been to a race start since 1982. When my son Mark ran the race in 1998 I went to the restart and helped him. I get invitations: "Why don't you come down?" I don't go. I was pretty old when I started. I think I was fifty on my last race and that was a Yukon Quest. I thought I was not doing as well as I should have because of aging. That's a tougher physical race than the Iditarod. I finished in the same place in two races and there was no point. It was a fun race, but I burned my snowshoes at the finish line in 1986 in Whitehorse. I burned the shoes, sold the dogs, and bought a sailboat.

My wife, Sandra, and I had the boat for ten years between 1988 and 1998. We were going to sail around Cape Horn and go to Seattle, but we got a call that my father had terminal cancer. So we put the boat on a big, flatbed truck and went over to Lake Michigan and spent a year at home until my dad passed away. The boat was a thirty-five-footer. We spent a year on the Gulf of Mexico and went to the Everglades. People talk about owning sailboats and owning dog teams the same way. You could have almost an identical conversation with a dog musher and just sub out the words. They always want to buy a bigger boat. But we didn't. For six years we never slept off the boat. We didn't pay for slips.

With dogs—and other mushers have said the same thing—there is always a point when you look out at the dog lot and you have to go one way or the other. You have to go all in or get out. It starts as a trapline team or a little recreational dog team, but when you reach a point there's always a reluctance to buy one more dog or spend money on one more thing. If you get all in, other priorities are completely out the window. If you get a new pair of shoes for yourself once a year that's good. But the rest of it has to go for the dogs in order to compete. If you're going to mush for more than entertainment, to compete, you have to be as obsessed about what you're doing as the people you're competing against. Otherwise there is no point in racing. And some of these people are really obsessed with what they're doing.

You can only put in 110 percent for so long and then you have to back off. In that era of the early 1980s I was competing against Rick Swenson and some other people who were very good at what they were doing. You had to be as crazy as they were in order to compete against them. Some mushers stayed in it forever and some saw no point in staying in forever. Once you accomplish what you set out to accomplish, why try to do it again because it's just going to be a disappointment? That's the way I felt about it. After 1980 there was no reason for me to be in the Iditarod anymore. Dean Osmar, when he won in 1983, same thing. Dean finished the race and someone asked him, "Are you going to come back and defend it next year?" He had a classic answer. He said, "What for?"

Where I live now in Trapper Creek I have one dog. I had someone else's dogs one winter and I trained them for her. I do not miss feeding dogs. If I'm not going to be racing, there's not much point. It comes up a lot to me that I won the Iditarod, but some people make it the whole center point of their life. I had a life before the Iditarod and a life after the Iditarod. It was a personal accomplishment. The winner's trophy ended up in a bar and the bar went out of business.

I had some mementoes from the race. They were from parts of races that I remember and parts of the race that I value because of some of the friends I made out there. The friendships don't go away. Those stay with you. And good memories. The good memories stay with you.

Grandpa, poster, 2007.

CHAPTER 9

Jon
VAN ZYLE

ertainly Jon Van Zyle has painted myriad pictures of mountains, wildlife, fishing, and Alaska landscapes, but he is famed for his decades-long association with the Iditarod, an event he loves.

Probably Alaska's most famous living artist, Van Zyle not only continues to release a popular poster for each Iditarod race, something he began as a fund-raiser for the Iditarod in the 1970s, but he is a veteran musher who twice completed the race and these days, along with his wife, Jona, still raises huskies and entertains tour groups that visit his Chugiak, Alaska, kennel.

Van Zyle's passion and commitment to the Iditarod earned him recognition in being selected for the *Anchorage Daily News* Iditarod Hall of Fame. The official Iditarod artist completed the race in 1976 in thirty-third place and in 1979 in forty-second place and he has painted dozens, if not hundreds, of dog-mushing scenes.

In recent years Van Zyle has also become a prolific illustrator of children's books about Alaska and other topics.

Growing up in Colorado, Van Zyle was always around dogs of some kind. His mother raised working collies, though he did not confuse them with Lassie. He appreciated working dogs the most after watching the collies herd sheep. Van Zyle believes he got his first husky in 1963 before he even moved to Alaska while he was attending junior college in Colorado.

I actually started racing dogs in the states, in California, Oregon, and Washington in the mid-1960s. They were sled dogs running with wheeled rigs. There was not a lot of snow. The races were short, six miles, ten miles, because of the heat. Even in the winter in Oregon it's still pretty warm. In Oregon there was some racing near Mount Hood.

My job was working for Sears and supervising construction of new stores, so I did a lot of traveling. I traveled with five or six dogs. It got to be a lot and I went to my boss at the time and said, "You know, I've always wanted to go to Alaska." I was supposed to have built the Anchorage store, but another guy lucked out and got the store. The Sears store was already built when I came to Alaska to work for it.

So I already had five or six dogs when I got to Alaska and a couple of years later I met Dick Mackey and Joe Redington and I was with a friend of mine, Bill Reynolds, at Tudor Track. They stopped by and asked if I would distribute some posters about this race that was going to happen. That was the first Iditarod in 1973 and we talked about it and it sounded interesting.

In fact, I was supposed to run it in 1975. I had made the arrangements with Sears to take the month off and the whole nine yards. I was an executive so I could kind of plan my own time. At the last minute I was told I couldn't do it, so a few months later I said the heck with the job. And I did the 1976 race.

I had been doing traveling with the dogs for several years before the Iditarod came along. I never liked the speed racing because it was over so quickly. I took camping trips and then when I heard about the Iditarod it just fit my idea of mushing. I suppose it was life altering. It was a great thing to have happen and it gave me some sort of direction, if not in art, at least for a period of time in my art.

I was always really dedicated to the art and only art I had physically experienced. I never wanted to paint something that was just made up and not experienced. I really don't know where that came from. I don't know where that idea or ideal comes from. My mother, Ruth, had an influence. She taught me to paint what I know.

Once I left Sears I became a full-time artist. My first Iditarod poster was 1977, the year after I first entered the race, and I have done one every year since. When I started it was just to give the Iditarod some money. The race didn't have any money. Like three guys and a dog knew about it. So it was to give them some exposure because I was starting to be published with reproduction prints. I had learned how to promote that kind of thing; I thought it would be a good way to help them. I still want to do it. My first one is probably my favorite, just because it is the first one and I didn't think there would be whatever it is, thirty-eight, thirty-nine, or forty of them. Another favorite was the 1985 poster because it showed one of my favorite dogs. It's a head shot of a dog.

Another favorite is from 1983 that has the phrase *Alone On the Crest of Your Dreams*. I had a really good friend who was my kennel partner and we trained dogs and traveled together and we were talking on the phone after I had done the painting. I was stuck for a title. In 1979, my second Iditarod, Gene Leonard from Finger Lake came in last and that's him on the poster with the red lantern. Gene had been a real mainstay of the race since the beginning and was just a real tough old guy, a solid kind of guy and I figured it made sense. The first poster cost $5. Now they're $38.

In the very beginning it was a poster and there was no signature on it. But we took a portion of those and we signed and numbered them. They were only in my gallery in Anchorage. The following year I was called by a lady and she said, "I noticed that there was a signed and numbered poster and there were several with all the same number." We went and investigated and sure enough there was a young man in the back room at the gallery forging my signature with a number like 77/500 or something like that. But the same number. Not very smart. It's a good thing that he did that or we would never have discovered it. They never received another image from Van Zyle. They weren't even thinking.

In 1983 I started issuing Iditarod prints, as well. It was a different image and it was a numbered edition. It was a dog team that had fallen through the ice and the musher is picking a dog up out of the ice and it was called *Close Call*. And there's been one ever since. Between the posters and the prints that's like seventy. Good God! That's a lot. But I'm not about to start on basketball. Didn't play. I wrestled, but didn't play basketball.

At this point in my career I have to paint about eighty paintings a year to keep everybody happy. About thirty of those are for kids' books and fifty are regular gallery paintings. I don't normally start the Iditarod projects until, I hate to say the last minute, but it is the last minute. It's already winter when I start it. But doing the Iditarod poster and print has become a smaller part of what I do all year long. It's not a major part of making a living, but I still want to do it. Heck, yeah. I am seventy-one years old, so I'm not going to do the Iditarod again, but I still like to be part of the Iditarod.

Mostly my travel along the Iditarod Trail is in my head. I've had a lot of surgeries and I stopped doing the Iditarod in 1979 for two reasons. One was that my career had taken off to the point where I was traveling a lot and I could not train dogs and travel. The other reason I stopped was that I saw changes coming in the race that were inevitable about speed and professionalism and that wasn't why I was running the Iditarod. It wasn't a camping experience anymore, but was more about speed, a lot more speed.

The inevitability was that it was a race that rewarded you for going faster, so it was going to get faster. In the early years, though, we managed to keep the racing and the speed—I don't want to say, in check—but it wasn't as big a deal. The big deal was starting in Anchorage and just getting to the end when there was no trail.

There have been tremendous changes, but the Iditarod, 100 percent, is still the most important thing for the people of Alaska. I don't know whether that will continue because I see changes in the generation coming up, the kids coming up, who really know nothing of the history of America and the history of Alaska, nor do they care.

More Alaskans still have a subsistence lifestyle than in any other state, but young people are growing up with computers and there are all these reality TV shows about Alaska that present a certain picture. The good thing is that they are built around the woodsmanship and romance of Alaska. Alaska still always gets the transplants from other places. They get tired of the rat race, living in the big city. I don't mean to make this sound arrogant, but the ones with forethought, with brains, they're tired of living the way they live. The appeal of Alaska is still "The Last Frontier."

I've been in Alaska for forty years, but I look at the 1970s as being modern Alaska already. That's not true of kids today. They think of the seventies the way I thought of the forties in the seventies. I guess everything is relative. We didn't have color TV. We didn't predict the Internet. Having the Internet means computers are an educational benefit to kids in the Bush and at the same time it puts them in touch with what the latest music is.

You can still live a somewhat rustic lifestyle in Alaska in the Bush with dogs if you have the wherewithal and finances to do it. You can't always make the finances work living out there. You practically have to have an endowment from which you can draw. You can make a few bucks selling furs, but that doesn't pay for a thousand gallons of fuel or gas to fly an airplane if you're a pilot. It's really hard and it always has been, but not as complicated as it is today.

It's harder than ever to be a dog musher training for the Iditarod if you don't live on the road system, even more today than yesterday. That's because back then we were all feeding our dogs fish and game. We weren't using commercial dog food. Now if you are not feeding commercial dog food you can't compete and you've got to buy it in town and ship it out. You can still feed fish, but you're not going to be competitive, not going to be in the top ten.

I was never a great competitor anyway when I did the Iditarod. My idea of doing the Iditarod was not being competitive. That was completely off my radar. I wanted to be there with the dogs and the art, to experience the country. There are still people who enter the Iditarod to do it and there are those who are out to win. I definitely don't think they should split it up into two classes, though. That to me is completely unacceptable. No, the Iditarod should never be closed to anyone entering who just wants to win a belt buckle. Period. I don't think the Iditarod should ever be so rigid where that person is excluded. They should never put the person who just wants to travel and see the country into a "lower" category. That's not what it was about in the beginning. I am totally against two classes, travelers and racers.

The belt buckle represents the accomplishment of getting there, no matter who you are. Some of the contenders could have been travelers at one time. Are they going to deny them? I don't think so. You've got people who come back every year who are good dog drivers, but who aren't going to win. They just take the trip, which is nice. We help sponsor various people. Karen Ramstead, for one. I don't know how much we help, but we try to. We're helping sponsor Lisbet Norris, the granddaughter of Earl and Natalie Norris [the famed old-time Alaska dog-mushing family].

The appeal of dog mushing has been there around the country in certain ways for a long time. They had the dog races in Laconia, New Hampshire. There were races in upstate New York and eastern Canada. Jona was racing in Ohio for twenty years. A large percentage of the American population has no clue, but it's always been a niche sport. The Iditarod just happened to tap into that and got lucky. And my art has, as well.

I was painting scenic art before the Iditarod stuff. I was painting a few dog teams. But somewhere along the line once the Iditarod poster got going that opened up a little bit broader audience. That attracted publishers for the prints. Fred Machetanz helped and he didn't even know it [with dog paintings] and galleries in California and Seattle helped me. The old saying is north of forty-seven degrees, or whatever, everybody knows somebody else.

About six years ago we were approached by a company called Entrée. They had an Entrée Canada and they were an offshoot company called Entrée Alaska. They heard of us, I'm assuming, through the art. The tourists we get are called "the Gucci crowd." They are mostly Americans, but a lot of them are from Europe. And they are wealthy. They come in limousines. They are small groups, high-end tours. We spend a half an hour or forty-five minutes in the dog lot. Our dog lot is clean, perfect, and the dogs are super friendly. Jona and I speak a little Iditarod history. Then they come into my studio and tour it and they have a very nice lunch. It's May through August, occasionally into September, and a couple of days during Iditarod time. We also have a lot of tours that we give for Habitat for Humanity, maybe six a year.

I really do enjoy doing the tours. I was traveling so much and doing shows and I like to meet the people who like my art. Now I still get to do that, but not to the degree we used to. Now those people are coming to see me as opposed to us getting on a plane to see them. So that's a nice thing.

CHAPTER 10

Hobo
JIM

The singer-guitar player known throughout Alaska as Hobo
Jim spends most of his year in Alaska, but also retains con-
nections to Nashville, where he established himself as a
country singer before becoming Alaska's troubadour. Hobo Jim Varsos
is an Alaska legend and the author of one of the state's most popular and
famous songs. He is as closely identified with the Iditarod Trail Sled Dog
Race as the dogs.

Hobo Jim's signature song, one that is a must for any concert he plays in
Alaska, is "I Did the Iditarod Trail." The catchy tune is known to all and that
includes schoolchildren who are often introduced to it at a very young age
and can be seen dancing to it in their classrooms.

In a notable comment about the song, 1985 champion Libby Riddles
said she was listening to the Nome radio station KNOM on her way into the
community approaching the finish line when Hobo Jim's song came on the
air. Riddles said it seemed as if they were playing it just for her.

Also, when Iditarod founder Joe Redington Sr. passed away Hobo Jim
penned a tribute song called "Redington's Run" that has also become a
staple of the race and very popular in the mushing community. It wouldn't

be a prerace Iditarod banquet in Anchorage without Hobo Jim playing his tunes as the event gets underway.

If you see Hobo Jim performing or just walking around the streets chances are extremely high he will be wearing a cowboy hat—yet he is more likely to be singing about people who wear fur hats.

I do have a place in Nashville, Tennessee, but I am definitely an Alaska resident. About twenty-five years ago I took a job in Tennessee as a staff songwriter for Warner Brothers and MCA. I did that for about six hundred songs worth, but I quit doing it about six years ago.

It was a desk job really. It was getting up in the morning, going to an office, and usually cowriting with somebody. We did that from nine o'clock until lunch break and finished up between two and five then went home. It was commercial country music for other people. I had cuts by Etta James, George Jones, Janis Ian. That wasn't making my own music.

Now 90 percent of what I do is my Alaska music. The majority of my living is actually in Alaska. Writing Alaska songs has paid off more than being in Tennessee. I have lived on the Kenai Peninsula for forty-three years. I'm just over sixty years old. In the summers I'm based in Soldotna. I play three nights a week in Soldotna and then I go to Homer two nights a week and Sundays I play in Seward. Mondays I usually do fish camps or special gigs. I work seven days a week in the summer and sometimes I work doubles and triples. The Alaska State Fair in Palmer is the end of my season. I finish up on Labor Day weekend.

Then I'll do a couple of weeks in Germany and in the winter I'll be around Wasilla. I'll do a couple of weeks here and there in Alaska and Outside. And I'm always at the banquet. I don't think I've ever missed a banquet since I started. The Nome finisher's banquet is where I started in 1982. Then the following year, I think, I did the Anchorage banquet and the Nome banquet. I quit the Nome banquet for about fifteen years because of scheduling. Then about three years ago I started going back to Nome. The Iditarod song is what really kicked off my career.

There's not a single night since I've written that song that I haven't played it. What's interesting to me is that kids know the words to it in Germany and Japan. When I get on the Internet and see kids in those countries singing it, it's awesome. Now they teach it around the state as part of the curriculum. At the banquet in Anchorage I get all these schoolteachers who have come up from around the country to see the start who are coming up to me telling me they teach it to kids. It's kind of neat knowing the kids around the world know it. It really is a signature song for me. I've got a couple others tagging along, but I'd have to say it's probably the signature song. The demand is always there for it.

In the old days I had to stop and explain what the Iditarod was before I played the song. Now I just go out and sing. There's not a single day since I wrote that song that I haven't promoted the Iditarod.

That song opened up a whole new culture to me. I've become tight friends with Joe Redington, Susan Butcher, and Lance Mackey over the years because of it. I've run with Dean Osmar since I was eighteen. I ran dogs with Dick Mackey when he was living in Wasilla. I was bordering on that culture, but by getting into the Iditarod through the song I've really made great friends.

I was born in Lafayette, Indiana, but I don't remember a thing about it because we left when I was young. From there my family moved to Wisconsin. Then I went to Kentucky and spent a couple of years on the road, hitchhiking around, train riding, and that's when I got the name Hobo Jim.

In Florida I was playing in a bar at Jacksonville Beach and I had a fake ID because I was underage. A friend nicknamed me Hobo Jim because I was riding the freights and the name stuck on the streets. Pretty soon I started using the nickname and everybody knew me by that name when I came to Alaska. It was like "Mountain Bob" and "Whiskey Bill." Everybody had a nickname. At that time in Alaska, you didn't ask anyone what their real name was, you know. We all had a little past we were leaving behind us. I never planned on Hobo Jim being a stage name.

I was a commercial fisherman by day and I ended up on the stage all of the time, too. Everyone knew me as Hobo Jim so they put it on the greeter board as just Hobo Jim. Nobody knows my last name. I still remember the time in Homer after I'd been there about eight years and a police officer pulled me over and asked to see my license. The cop said, "I just wanted to know what your last name was." He didn't pull me over because I was speeding or anything—I was walking.

Looking back it figures that I came to Alaska. It's funny, I didn't know it, but I have roots here. It turned out that members of my mom's family have been in Seward since 1914, and I didn't even know it. I found out later.

That didn't have anything to do with me coming to Alaska, though. I met a girl in New Orleans and we started hitchhiking together. I usually hitched alone, but we hitched together and we went to her home in El Paso, Texas. Then she said she had a friend in Vancouver she wanted to see, so we hitched up there. When we got there we found out her friend had moved to Williams Lake, British Columbia, so we hitchhiked there. By the time we got there her friend had her bags packed and was heading to Alaska. We got to Alaska in January of 1972. I think we got here on January 3. Soldotna practically didn't exist and Homer was a quiet little town with fishing. We came to the Kenai Peninsula and initially stayed with someone in a cabin for a couple of months and then went to Homer, where I lived until about twenty-five years ago when I moved to Soldotna.

The "I Did the Iditarod Trail" song came up in an unusual way. I was scheduled to go to Nome for the end of the race in 1982 and sing at the Bering Sea Saloon. I was told that ABC-TV was going to be there filming and I ought to write a song and maybe I would get on the *20/20* show. I promised them I would have a song. They kept calling me and asking, "Did you get the song yet? Did you get the song yet?" I hadn't. They had already told the TV people that I had a song. I said, "I'll get it. I'll get it."

The night before my wife said, "You don't have it yet?" I said, "I'll get it." I was in bed sound asleep and I had a dream that I was writing. I jumped up and told my wife, "I've got it." She said, "What?" I said, "I did, I did, I did the Iditarod Trail." She looked at me and said, "Go back to bed." I got up in the morning and I just had it. It was all there.

I went down to the Soldotna Inn, took one of their placemats, wrote it all down, and off to Nome we went. I wrote it that night and it was on TV the next day.

Joe Redington put "I did, I did, I did the Iditarod Trail" on the back of his truck and that was kind of a big thrill. His wife, Vi, always used to love that song so much. Lance Mackey has told me many times how much he likes it. Rick Swenson told me. Everyone says they've heard it so many times at the Bering Sea. That made fans of it. When Joe died in 1999 I wrote another song called "Redington's Run." That has become a real requested song, too. Every night that I do it, it is in honor of Joe and I tell a story about who he was. Every night.

I'm not really a musher. I have friends who have dogs. I'd run with them. There is a race in Michigan called the Mackinaw Mush and I wrote the theme song for that, too, and I used to race in a celebrity mush there. Libby Riddles did it. Linwood Fiedler did it. Actually, Linwood and I would always race together for years and if I came in sixth he came in fifth. If I came in thirteenth he came in twelfth. He was always one spot ahead of me. One year no one brought their own dogs so we pieced together a team when we got there. Everybody packed together their worst dogs for Linwood and they got the best team they could for me. I left him smoking in the aisles. That's the only dog race I ever won.

Back in the peak early days of the song, I would say 1985 or 1986, everybody was pushing me to run the Iditarod and everybody offered me dogs to use. Joe Redington offered me dogs to use and Dick Mackey offered me dogs and Dean Osmar offered me dogs and Susan Butcher offered me dogs. I could have had a phenomenal team. I'm sure I wouldn't have been competitive in any way, but I could have had a great dog team. But I've always had poor hand circulation. My hands get cold really easily. I was worried about frostbitten fingers. I was doing all kinds of crazy things back then. That was in my bull wrestling days and my skydiving days. When my wife and I met I was working on Anchor Point and I did bull wrestling. That's what bull dogging is called.

In the rodeo, cowboys on horseback chase after the steers and wrestle them to the ground. The best of them weigh around 250 pounds, big guys, and I was wrestling at around 150. But I did pretty good. It wasn't as if I thought the Iditarod was too tough to do, but I was strictly worrying about my hands. Now that I'm older I realize how much protecting your hands means, especially when you play the guitar.

Long after I moved to Alaska I found out about the family in Seward. I remembered my grandmother getting postcards and letters from Alaska. My mother had them stashed in her cedar chest. She sent me photographs and a copy of the family tree. I was reading it and there was this family named Painter in Seward. The last entries were four children born in the 1920s. I thought surely someone was alive and I looked up directory information and found Roger Painter and talked to him.

My grandmother's sister was his mom. We talked and he didn't know anything beyond his mom and dad's family history. I had the whole tree and I had black-and-white pictures of him and his siblings when they were little kids standing in front of their cabin before it burned down in the 1920s or 1930s. I gave him a whole bunch of pictures and letters from his family that I think are now in the Seward Museum because they were homesteaders. He had a daughter who lived in Homer and I said, "I don't know her." He said she was married and had a different last name. It turned out she was one of my dear friends and we hadn't known it, but she was like my second cousin. We had been friends for years.

Now because of marriages and relationships everybody that has been on the Kenai Peninsula for any length of time has come out saying we're cousins. I married into the Leman family, former Lieutenant Governor Loren Leman. Alaska was a small place before World War II, so if you had any roots here and especially on the Kenai Peninsula, you could be related.

To me the Iditarod race is one of the last vestiges of Alaska. Once I get out of Anchorage, to McGrath—I've played McGuire's there lots of times— or Rainy Pass, or something like that, we're in village country. It just seems so Alaskan. People are wearing their beaver hats because that's what they wear, not because it's Anchorage Fur Rendezvous. They made them. When I get out there, and to Nome, I always feel like I still live in Alaska.

In the beginning years of the race, for me in the early 1980s, it was so colorful. We had the "Shishmaref Cannonball" and "Cowboy Smith." All of these colorful characters. To me, it's almost a shame that it went so commercial. When it got up to bigger money, and big sponsors, and big contracts, it became more of a sponsored event. It used to be just a guy and a few dogs that decided to take a run in the snow and race each other. It used to be just a bunch of locals getting their dogs together and racing them. Now it's more like the Indianapolis 500. Everything changes.

It's the same as the state growing. It's got its ups and downs and it's been good for me. Watching the state grow along with the Alaska Pipeline was distressing to me at times, but when I look at it now I wouldn't have had a career if it wasn't for that happening. You've got to learn to go with the kicks, I guess. If you get out of the state, when you leave and come back, it's only then you realize how different we still are from everyone else.

The Iditarod is still "The Last Great Race on Earth." There isn't anything like it. It's just an incredible race. To think that Lance Mackey can win the Yukon Quest and ten days later do the Iditarod. Tim Osmar won the Quest and my guitar has a gold nugget in it that comes from Timmy's halfway money. They gave him four ounces of gold nuggets in halfway money. He gave me a nugget from that race to imbed in my guitar.

That made it a true Alaskan guitar. I taught myself how to play guitar. I never had a lesson in my life. Just about everything came from just working at it. I've been writing songs since I was fifteen, but they weren't any good. When I first moved to Alaska I was just writing about what was around me, what I saw. I wasn't trying to get a hit song. I was just writing for the sake of writing.

Working in Nashville kind of took away my inspiration, but it made me a better writer, a better craftsman, but it took away the natural vein. I've been waiting for that spirit to come back fully. Finally it has and I'm doing a new album, the best Alaskan record I've ever written. It has "I Am Alaskan," one of the best Alaska things I've ever written. Some of it goes, "I am the raven's call from ancient cedars standing tall. I break the silence of the fog over icy waterfalls. I'm an eagle when he flies in clear blue sky. Here the sound of freedom's cry. I am Alaska."

I am much more of an Alaskan than someone from Nashville. I have no connection with Nashville at all. The only reason I kept the home there is because my boy lives there and my grandkids are around there. My wife doesn't like Alaska winters, either. Last year I spent maybe two months total in Nashville. One year I spent fourteen days there. I go there for visits.

I love every bit of being in Alaska and being around the Iditarod. I don't have to look for work anymore and I'm doing what I want to do more than I ever have in my life. I had just written a song called "Where Legends Are Born" about Alaska and when she was the speaker of the House of Representatives, Gail Phillips asked me if I could play it for the legislature. So I went to Juneau and played it at the opening session. Then I got an official title. I'm the "State Balladeer." The governor and legislature named me that in 1994.

One time or another, one way or another, I've played just about everywhere you can go in Alaska. I'm on the Kenai Peninsula in the summer where the tourists are, but winter is the time I get around the state. I go to Fairbanks a couple of times a year. I go to Kodiak a couple of times a year. I go to Juneau, Ketchikan, King Salmon, Pelican Island. There's probably hardly any place I haven't played in Alaska. I jump at a chance to play somewhere if there's hunting or fishing there. I'm doing more remote lodges. I've pretty much seen the whole state: Endicott, the Arctic National Wildlife Refuge, Iliamna, Dillingham, Whittier, Glennallen, Cordova, Dutch Harbor. Wait. I haven't been to St. Lawrence Island. There's one place left to go.

Moonlit Leader, print, 2008.

Karen
TALLENT

A longtime Iditarod volunteer, Karen Tallent of Anchorage represents the hundreds of race supporters who give their time each
year to making sure the one-thousand-mile race goes off like
clockwork. Volunteers are a critical element of the Iditarod, whether that is
in Anchorage at the ceremonial start, in Willow at the official restart, or at
every checkpoint along the trail, and at the finish line in Nome.

Tallent, a schoolteacher who is also a major Syracuse University basketball
fan, has been an Iditarod volunteer for years. Her efforts have almost exclusively
been in connection with the downtown Anchorage portion of the race. Tallent has rarely been on the trail and each March she generally follows the race
unfolding like most other fans—through television, newspaper, and the Internet.

She taught at Willow Crest Elementary School, Rogers Park Elementary School, and Dimond High School before parting with the Anchorage
School District.

By the time Tallent moved to Alaska in 1990 from Syracuse she was
already aware of the Iditarod, but not originally by following it. A handler
for 1984 Iditarod champion Dean Osmar was from Syracuse and he was
home visiting his family when Tallent met him at a folk concert and dance.

Two years after Tallent moved to Alaska she became an Iditarod volunteer, but by then she had already met some sled dogs.

I met Bill and I started dating him and came to Alaska to visit in the summer and met Dean Osmar and went out on the boat with the guys who were set netters. In 1990 I took some time off from teaching and went to work in the North Slope oil fields. One of my brothers worked for a company that sent him to the North Slope to feed everybody in 1989 and the company kept him here. He said, "I'll put you to work on the Slope." I moved to Alaska in July of 1990.

In 1991 I asked for time off to come into Anchorage to see the race start and after that I was hooked. The next year I volunteered. I got trained as a dog handler, worked the prestart getting the mushers parked in their spots, and then I volunteered in the phone room.

Working in the phone room was exciting because that was before everything was computerized with websites and the Internet. We had tons of phone calls. The minute you picked up a phone and answered a question, and put it down again, there was another call. It was just constant. A lot of it was race results. I would go to school during the day and work the phones at night. A lot of mushers' families called in those days to find out how their musher was doing. I talked a lot to Susan Butcher's mom. Of course she wanted to know how Susan was doing, but I was a teacher who taught special ed and worked with learning disabled students. We talked about that a lot. Susan was even on the *Oprah* show years ago and it was a show about women who had overcome obstacles in their lives to be very successful in their field. She talked about her learning disability. Her mom and I sort of had that connection.

Then kids would call from their schools in the Lower 48 and the whole class would get on the phone. Each kid would have one question to ask. There might be thirty of them and so you're on the phone for an hour talking with the class. They called from all across the country and they each had their own questions. They were following certain mushers and they wanted to know what kind of equipment the mushers carried in their sleds. They wanted to know about the checkpoints, the dogs, and the weather. It was fun talking to the classrooms.

Then I worked on press conferences and the mushers' banquet. Once, I went out to McGrath with two other volunteers and cooked. We cooked for all of the volunteers, the mushers who scratched, the pilots, the veterinarians, and when there was free time I helped out in the dog lot a little bit. It was lots of fun. All of my years with the Iditarod has been fun times.

Most of what I have done is in Anchorage at the start and then I went to the restart when it was in Wasilla and then to Willow when it switched there. I might get a couple of hours sleep on Friday and then be downtown in Anchorage by 5 A.M. Saturday for the staging on the streets before the ceremonial start because my volunteers would come at 5:30. We were there before the mushers brought their trucks in. Then the next day I would drive out to the restart and help out there. I wouldn't have time to go out on the trail because I was teaching. There's always work. I always had to be at work on Monday.

I've helped organize the shipments of food drops to mushers at the checkpoints and I've overseen the packaging of hay drops to go out to the checkpoints. Mark Nordman (race marshal) always said, "You've done so many things, whenever you want to go out on the trail, just let me know." I've done an awful lot of different jobs, but mostly in Anchorage. Now that I am no longer boxed into a regular schedule with my job, I can get out on the trail.

Instead of working in the schools I am a studio teacher. That means I work with children who are in films, TV shows, and commercials. I get to teach and work with kiddos, but not in a regular classroom. Projects come up at different times, but I never have a set schedule. This is when movies are made in Alaska and I've done some great movies and TV shows. I worked on the movie *Big Miracle* and we had a ten-year-old fifth-grader from Rabbit Creek Elementary School who had a major role and who had never acted before. Ahmaogak Sweeney was chosen for the role. His mom is Iñupiaq from Barrow. I worked the whole movie with him.

Ahmaogak was the best kid in the world. Smart, confident, and funny, a typical ten-year-old boy, but he had to have schooling because the movie started filming in September and finished at the end of November. I did schooling with him every day and I was always with him on the set. As the student's teacher you also have to make sure the child labor laws are followed, so you keep track of his hours.

It has been very interesting. You're on location. Another time I worked on a commercial for Samsung with a Korean film crew and we were at the top of the Knik Glacier. It started off really nice and then the weather came in. The pilot was saying, "We've got to go. We've got to go." We were throwing gear and wardrobes into the plane before we got stuck there. They only had one day to get the commercial filmed, so we had to go back out there after the weather cleared. Then they couldn't find everything they needed because we had left so quickly. The Koreans started screaming at one another and punching each other in the head and I've got this six-year-old kid up there. I said, "Stop! Let's just film this and be done." It was crazy.

You never know what is going to happen. But *Big Miracle* was a great experience and Ahmaogak and his family were wonderful. I haven't had a chance yet to work on a movie about the Iditarod or a dog-sled movie. That would be the ultimate. There is some talk, though, about making a movie from the book *The Cruelest Miles*, which is about the 1925 serum run, and of it being filmed in Alaska. There would be a lot of Alaska kiddos in that.

McGrath is really the only place in the middle of the trail that I have been. I did get to Nome once for a finish in the late 1990s when Jeff King won and DeeDee Jonrowe finished second. I saw the first fifteen mushers come in. I spent three days in Nome with no sleep. There is no sleep during the Iditarod in Nome. You're in the bars until 5 A.M. with the sponsors and the pilots, the volunteers, and the mushers' families. It was just so much fun. I volunteered in the finisher's chute and that was so much fun, too. After three days with no sleep I had to go back to Anchorage. I never expected it to be so emotional to see those fifteen mushers come into Nome. I always sent them off at the start in Anchorage, or the restart in Wasilla or Willow, but I was just crying when Jeff came in.

Jeff had come through a bad storm and he was exhausted. He was just frozen, his beard, his eyelashes, everything was frozen and I just started to cry. I couldn't believe it. It was, "Oh, my God, he's made it." It was just like the most incredible journey and for once I got to see it. I was there at the beginning and I was there at the end. That was really cool.

I have been a volunteer with the Iditarod for more than twenty years and I'm not ready to give it up. Sometimes when I'm operating on a couple of hours of sleep during the race I think, *Why do I still do this?* But I absolutely love it. It's just such a unique event. The people, the mushers that do this are very special people. There is really only a select small group of people that could go all these miles with the dogs in these incredible weather conditions.

The dogs are amazing. As a dog handler they just want to lick you and be loved and they're so happy. They don't know me from Jack, but they're the sweetest, most wonderful animals to be around, and they are real athletes.

I've met so many wonderful people over the years and not just Alaskans, but people from Outside and international places. There have been people from Australia or Norway, and journalists who have come through just for press conferences. When there was a Japanese musher we had Japanese press people. It's a combination of everything that makes it so neat.

It's happened a lot, right back to the beginning, that a volunteer becomes a musher. Bill Cotter was a checker in the very first Iditarod and he had a long mushing career, but that's what got him going. Being a dog handler for the start and restart I thought I should really learn more about mushing and one year I was a handler in the chute.

When Peryll Kyzer was still running—she was a goat farmer, and a really neat person—I happened to be a holder for her team and she was going to check on all of her dogs and they're counting down, ten, nine, eight, and I'm on the sled with my feet on the brake and they're going, five, four, three, two, one and she's still checking out her dogs. I'm thinking, *I'm not taking these puppies to Nome*. I'm going, *Peryll, Peryll, it's time to go*. Then I handled for her at the restart and she wanted me to help put harnesses and booties on the dogs. I thought, *Well, if I'm going to be around these dogs like this I need to know more*. So I took a mushing class at the University of Alaska Anchorage. We spent time in the classroom learning about the whole breeding process and everything about sleds and equipment and then went to a kennel. Then we got to take dogs out to the Birchwood dog track and run them. It was me and a classmate with one sled and four dogs and we had to harness the dogs, bootie them, and feed and water them. You don't just stand on the sled runners. You lean to the right and to the left. There are so many things to be aware of. You give commands. It was exciting and exhilarating and I thought, *Now I know why people mush dogs*.

It was just for a few miles, but afterwards I called my husband, Randy, and I said, "Oh, my God, we've got to get dogs. We've got to buy a sled so I can run the Iditarod." He was just laughing. It was so exciting, but then reality set in. It didn't happen.

Everyone in Alaska loves the event. They love the mushers. They love the dogs. It's the highlight of winter. Winters are long and dark and cold here in Alaska, but we absolutely love our mushers and dogs and Iditarod. We know the mushers by their first names. It's personal. They're our neighbors. Every year you're interested in how DeeDee Jonrowe is going to do. "Is DeeDee going to win?" When Libby [Riddles] won and Susan [Butcher] won I loved that T-shirt about Alaska, where men are men and women win the Iditarod. It's time for another woman to win. I need a new T-shirt.

All the years I was volunteering when I was in the school system I would get asked all kinds of questions about the Iditarod. The schools are a great place for Iditarod volunteers. I was just getting hooked. It was exciting to be around the pandemonium and other people were curious about what it was like. In the precomputer age teachers would ask, "Hey, who's in the lead?" or "What's going on?" During a break in the middle of the day I would call the phone room and get the latest information.

One year in the early 1990s, right before the Anchorage start, we had a murder downtown. The body in a car ended up at Fourth and D Streets, right at the starting line. This was early morning, a few hours before the start. The streets are sealed off, but there was a car where the road had been closed. The actual shooting had been at H Street and they were fleeing and the body and the car ended up in a snow berm. Everything was set up for the race and the starting line became a murder scene. Now I show up to organize the start. It was 4:45 in the morning and I was lost in thought about everything that had to be done.

I was waiting for thirty-five or forty people for the start and I just duck under this yellow tape and I think, Oh, that's weird. We didn't put this here. What is this yellow tape? It was police yellow crime scene tape. I look up and a whole bunch of policemen are rushing towards me. They ask, "Who are you and what are you doing here?"

So I tell them my name and I'm here to set up for the race and one of them goes, "Well, little lady, we're gonna have to rain on that parade." I go, "What? The race is going to start in a few hours." They were dragging the body out of the car and I'm going, "Oh, my God." We always kept an RV parked on the street once we set up for people to sleep in and keep an eye on things. I had to go wake them up at 5 A.M. and they had missed the whole thing. They didn't hear or see anything. Because the actual murder took place on H Street we couldn't use that whole north side of the street. Mushers were supposed to be parked there. I had to call the city, get them to come in and lay down snow on the south side of the street. We put up snow fencing. One of my volunteers stapled his hand to the snow fencing with one of those big, industrial-sized guns and I had to get the EMTs for him. Then I had all of the press coming to me because they wanted to interview Rick Swenson and DeeDee Jonrowe and they weren't where the map said they were supposed to be.

A lot of the mushers were delayed getting to their spots and I had a communication walkie-talkie and I'm getting calls from mushers getting on the radio saying if we don't get them parked in the next so many minutes there's going to be another murder on the Iditarod Trail. This is after Sue Henry's book *Murder on the Iditarod Trail* had come out. I couldn't help but laugh. It was just so perfect. The mushers were getting really antsy because it was getting close to nine o'clock. The police took the body away before the dogs came down the street, but they were looking for shotgun casings and things like that.

I'm fifty-nine and I live in South Anchorage, in the city, so I don't think I'm about to start mushing now. It's a whole lifestyle and I don't really have a spot for dogs. Your whole life is dogs. I grew up in Syracuse and I went to Syracuse University, so I really root for the basketball team. They're always in the NCAA tournament and they always have playoff games in March at the same time as the Iditarod. Sometimes they play games on the same day as the Iditarod starts. I get up even earlier to make sure I set the recorder for the game before I go volunteer for the Iditarod.

It's not going to happen that I become a musher racing in the Iditarod, but I will be a volunteer forevermore.

CHAPTER 12

Jake
BERKOWITZ

*T*he outdoors has always been in Jake Berkowitz's blood, growing up in Minnesota and living in Michigan's Upper Peninsula. By the age of eighteen he decided he wanted to become an Iditarod musher and guided sled-dog trips in the Lower 48, where he had also been an avid canoer and backpacker. He made his Iditarod debut at age twenty-two in 2008 and in 2009 he moved to Alaska.

Berkowitz and his wife, Robin, have one child, Ruby, and they live in Big Lake, Alaska. At twenty-eight he was regarded as one of the sport's up-and-coming mushers, but after pouring his heart and soul into the race for a decade he had second thoughts about his commitment after the 2014 race.

After founding Apex Kennels, Berkowitz impressed mushing observers by finishing the Iditarod with all sixteen dogs in harness during his first try, and by winning several middle-distance races, including the Copper Basin 300.

Berkowitz was rookie of the year in the Yukon Quest and in 2013 won the Iditarod's Humanitarian Award. Along with Iditarod champion John Baker, as a summer job Berkowitz provides sled-dog rides for $10 a shot and educational instruction on mushing at the Alaska Native Heritage Center in Anchorage. In 2013, Berkowitz placed eighth in the Iditarod for his best overall finish to date. That was his third finish and represented by far his fastest time on the one-thousand-mile route.

At six feet tall and weighing around 240 pounds, Berkowitz has been one of the sport's largest contending mushers. Being of lighter weight is considered to be an advantage because it means less for the dogs to pull. Berkowitz was one of the victims of the rugged trail in the 2014 race, breaking his sled to bits and being forced out of the race early.

Having a young child, coupled with striking out in that race, made him reevaluate his long-term plans and after the race he sold his dog team and is leaving long-distance mushing behind—at least for a while. Berkowitz is far from the only Iditarod musher to choose family time and trying to make more money over sticking with the sport.

My grandfather actually raised dogs, though not sled dogs. I've had dogs my whole life, starting with growing up in Minnesota. I grew up in the city, St. Paul, but my entire childhood I spent summers in the Boundary Waters, then I actually ended up guiding white-water canoe trips. Once, we actually did a sixty-day Arctic expedition going out of Yellowknife in the Northwest Territories. That was an amazing experience. There are a lot of intrepid explorers in the Boundary Waters. I love it there. If we were ever to move away from Alaska we would probably go to Ely, Minnesota.

Once, I was looking for a winter guiding job and I got on a Greyhound bus and got a job in Michigan with Iditarod musher Ed Stielstra. In my third year I actually ran an Iditarod team for him, finishing in 2008. Then I got a job offer from Zack Steer [third in the 2007 race] and Bob Bundtzen. I came here to run my second Iditarod and that was the year I was fortunate to finish with sixteen dogs. We were in Nome and they just offered me a job. They were looking for a new handler. Bob wanted a new handler. He's a full-time doctor and he needed a full-time handler in order to train. They told me it was going to be lots of dogs and long, long hours. I ended up training thirty-eight dogs primarily myself for two Iditarod teams that year.

I stayed in Anchorage for two months, trucking the dogs to Chugiak every day and once the training miles got longer I moved out to Sheep Mountain where Zack had his lodge. Then Zack offered me a job for the following year training his team for the Iditarod and the Yukon Quest. I ran my 2009 Iditarod out of Sheep Mountain Lodge and then I trained Zack's 2010 Quest and

Iditarod team out of Sheep Mountain Lodge. After I spent the two seasons with Zack and Bob, Jon Little [fourth in the 2002 race] called me up and offered me his kennel. He was leaving Alaska and giving up mushing to move to Texas.

I respect Jon a lot. Money wasn't an issue for him. He really believed in his line of dogs and he wanted to see a young musher that he knew take them over. I had run some of Jon's dogs in the Iditarod. He lent me some of the really young dogs to keep that line going and I promised him that we would keep that line of dogs going and bring them to new heights. I stay in contact with him. I call him after every race.

So I bought a piece of property, took twenty-eight dogs from Jon, and began building up Apex Kennels. We've been fortunate. That first year racing my own dogs we ended up setting a record in the Copper Basin [race]. My team won the Northern Lights 300. We ran the Fur Rondy. We were having fun. I was fortunate enough to get good dogs and we bonded quickly. This was my full-time job.

My family in Minnesota kind of marvels that this is who I am. They come up and visit. My dad and my wife's father, my father-in-law, helped handle the first part of the Yukon Quest. My mom and dad have been to the start of the Iditarod. My dad's been to Nome. They love it. They love the lifestyle and they love the dogs. They were definitely concerned in 2000 when I loaded up on that Greyhound bus on a Thanksgiving weekend and headed out. There wasn't even a bus stop where they dropped me off. They just dropped me off on the side of a gravel road. I got on the bus in St. Paul, Minnesota, and they dropped me off at a street lamp in the Upper Peninsula of Michigan. I waited there for maybe an hour. I was just standing there. One of Ed Stielstra's handlers picked me up.

My first experience with the dogs in Michigan was arriving at like five in the morning in the pitch black to a kennel with about a hundred dogs and all you could hear was the dogs barking and howling. The light came up and suddenly you could see them. It was a magical type entry into what the rest of my life has turned into.

The first time I ran the Iditarod was 2008 and I finished sixty-fifth. My first Iditarod was rough. My first Iditarod was a race I don't wish on anyone. I think I brought seven dogs into Nome. It was kind of one injury after the other. The saying is true that you've got to be in Alaska to really learn how to run dogs and run the Iditarod. I had come from Michigan. I had not seen the majority of that terrain. It was a great eye-opener. It was one of my proudest moments to finish. I was down to ten dogs in Ophir and eight dogs in Elim and if I didn't finish that race I don't think I would be where I am right now. It's pretty easy to throw in the towel and call it quits. Scratching was never an option. We just kept going. I knew I was going to finish.

It was very memorable and an important stepping-off point. If I didn't finish that race I probably wouldn't have had the job with Zack and Bob the next year. I was looking for another job. As soon as I got to the finish line Ed kind of thought, *Oh, he's never going to run another Iditarod.* Then he did offer me the job again and I weighed my options between Ed and Zack and Bob and I chose Zack and Bob in Alaska. It's been a great friendship. Bob was selling his old guard. I actually bought three of his dogs and two of them were in my winning Copper Basin team. It's been a great friendship and a great relationship.

That first race was a huge learning experience for me and it was really necessary. I fell in love with the sport. I always was a competitive kid, always in competitive sports. I was captain of my tennis team. I played basketball and soccer. I was in swimming. I loved competition. My parents were competitive people. My grandfather at eighty-five still plays tennis. My mom was a college tennis player. My dad played soccer in college. I don't think I won my first Chutes and Ladders game at home until I actually won. They made sure that I knew that winning didn't come easy and you deserve to win when you do win. You've got to earn it.

I learned how little I knew in my first Iditarod and I'm still learning how little I know. You learn something every Iditarod. In 2013 we got hit in an insane storm. The front five of us at the time, going to Kaltag and Unalakleet, got hit with a monster blizzard that no one else got hit by. So the Iditarod is demanding. It's a massive chess game where not everyone is on a level playing field because of the weather. That's what makes the Iditarod. That's what makes you come back every year, knowing your dog team and seeing how you can conquer the different weather each year.

What distinguishes my first Iditarod the most was my inexperience and getting down to only seven dogs. Maybe that's why I finish with so many dogs now. Over the past few Iditarods I dropped only three dogs. In 2009, my second Iditarod, I took all sixteen to Nome. Twelve of those were only sixteen-month-olds. Then I took two years off, the first year to help Zack

Steer and the second year to build up my kennel and run middle-distance races. I came back in 2012, but unfortunately I had to pull out in Unalakleet. I was withdrawn in Unalakleet because I put a knife through my left hand severing the artery. It's good now, but it gets cold easily. It was hard for me withdrawing. I think I was in fifteenth place in Unalakleet and still had fourteen dogs. I was separating fish about twenty-five miles from Unalakleet when I did it.

I don't think the accident was sleep induced. It was something that I had done a thousand times and this time the knife just slipped. We all separate fish [break up frozen chunks] with our knives. It's probably not the smartest thing, but we do a lot of dumb things out there on the Iditarod that we're not supposed to do. I was just separating fish and the knife just twisted and went right into the hand.

It had been a really warm race and then it got super cold. It was about minus forty when I cut my hand. All of my precut fish had frozen back together looking like a whole fish. I was just separating it. That was an "Oh, shit" moment. I knew I was probably done with the race right then. I did not want anyone to come out and rescue me, so I knew I had to get to Unalakleet [about three hundred miles from the end of the race]. I ended up having some veterinarian wraps in the sled that we can use basically to stop bleeding or holding something tight on a dog. I just wove the vet wrap really tight and tied off the artery with a pressure bandage and made it to Unalakleet. It was obvious I wouldn't be able to continue in the race. It wasn't one of those decisions where I was arguing with the race judge that I could keep going. It was in the best interests of my team and myself that I pulled out at that point. Mark Nordman, the race marshal, withdrew me, but I didn't contest it. That was hard leaving my dog team, but I got flown into Anchorage.

The race I finished with sixteen dogs was 2009. When you're at White Mountain getting close to the end [seventy-seven miles away] sixty-four booties is a lot of booties to put on. My goal that year was not to win the Iditarod. My goal was not to be in the top thirty. My goal was to take the young dogs for Bob and Zack to Nome and get as many of them there as possible. We had huge storms on the Yukon River that year. That year we had one-hundred-mile-per-hour gusts on the Yukon so it was a real honor getting those dogs through that storm and not dropping any. There weren't even parking spaces in most of the villages on the Bering Sea Coast that were big enough for sixteen dogs. I remember when we stopped my team was all pretzeled in.

You don't expect to have that many dogs left at that point. I actually had to be buying booties. Zack had told me, "Let's not even send out sixteen sets of booties to the Coast because there's no way you're going to have that many dogs." So I'm sitting there bartering with people to buy booties off of them. I had cash. I had a lot of fish.

Ed Stielstra and I were actually traveling together. It was kind of fun to actually beat the guy that you had run a team for the year before. But I was giving him fish. They don't have fish down in Michigan. So I was giving him fish and he was giving me booties. There were two dogs in that team, Duster and Hugo, that were actually fourteen months old. I don't think I've ever heard of any dogs younger than that finishing the Iditarod. They're six years old now.

I went to the Quest because I had to expedite my learning curve. I knew I couldn't spend ten years trying to get into the top ten in the Iditarod. I didn't have the money and I didn't have the desire. I wanted to get to the top as fast as possible and the best way to do that is to gain experience. The best way to do that is running multiple one-thousand-mile races and different one-thousand-mile races. It's also kind of my philosophy that you can't be a long-distance sled driver and claim you're a long-distance sled driver without running both the Yukon Quest and the Iditarod.

We named our baby girl *Ruby* and while that's a checkpoint on the northern route of the Iditarod it was actually my grandmother's name. I really like the northern route. I look forward to seeing those villages, Ruby, Galena, Nulato. That's one thing the Quest lacks. There's a lot more wilderness. I really enjoy the village style. That's the reason I go to the Kuskokwim 300 and the Kobuk 440: I love the Native races. There's more Alaskan flavor. I've made lifelong friends coming into the villages. I wouldn't change me running two Iditarods with young teams. I was able to spend more time in the villages with people. Now we're racing so hard you don't stop very long.

You really understand that no matter how tired and grumpy you are coming into a village that there are lot of people there really excited to see you and who have put a lot of time and energy into putting on this race. You've got to put all of the problems you've had on that run behind you and put on a good show for Iditarod and for all the people who make it possible.

I've spent seven years working with the public through tourism. When September rolls around we're training dogs full-time. My summertime is not only about making money, but we have a huge fan base. It's really about bringing dog sledding to the public. You know the misnomer about how we're forcing these dogs to run across Alaska. It's education, especially at the Alaska Native Heritage Center. They're not coming specifically for a dog ride. They get to the center and they're excited that we're here. I think we've done a really good job across Alaska through tourism combating that idea that we're forcing dogs to run. People see that we don't have a motor on our cart. There's nothing dragging the dogs along. When I whistle the team jumps up and starts barking and the dogs are going crazy to go. It's been a really rewarding experience how many new fans we create for Iditarod every year just through the tourism business in the summertime.

A common remark that people make is that they thought the dogs would be bigger. I'm never going to be a featherweight on the sled. When you look at our dogs you'll see that we have one of the larger dog teams, too. My males average about sixty-five pounds and I have some females in my team that are about fifty-five pounds, so being a big guy doesn't hurt us.

We're trying to get them [fans] away from that preconceived notion of Disney dogs. The Hollywood version of sled dogs is Siberian huskies and malamutes. I tell everyone that yes they are sled dogs, but you are never going to win the Iditarod with them. They're kind of your Brad Pitts and Angelina Jolies of the dog world. They're very pretty and that's why they're in the movies. These are your hockey players, the guys that you throw in and they get the job done.

In 2013 I ended up finishing the race with fifteen dogs and I received the Humanitarian Award. That was a huge honor and one that you might win just once in your career. I know a lot of people in this race for twenty-five years who have never gotten it.

Our goal is to win the Iditarod. Going into the 2014 race I had twenty-eight dogs that had finished the Iditarod or the Quest. They were all three years old to six years old. I was fourth into Unalakleet in 2013, but I did not honestly believe that I could win the Iditarod that year. I knew I could be top four. To win the Iditarod you can never doubt it. John Baker taught me that. Never doubt yourself that you can win the Iditarod.

It became a reality that I was not going to win the Iditarod and at that point I made the decision for a goal to finish with as many dogs as possible, be in the top ten, and hopefully get the Humanitarian Award. From Unalakleet on that was my goal and I stuck to it. I've spoken at some Iditarod rookie meetings and I tell them to know their goal and know their limits. If you think you have a top-twenty dog team run at a top-thirty pace and chances are you will finish fifteenth. If you bring a team that's a top-thirty team and you race for a top-twenty finish you're going to fall on your face and probably finish fortieth. You need to be realistic with your goals.

You need to know your dogs' limits and you need to know your limits. You need to race within your abilities or you're going to blow yourself away in the Iditarod. For two Iditarods I had the slowest times into Skwentna by a long shot. It's a thousand-mile race and the way I run my first seventy miles isn't dictating how I am going to run the rest of my race. People may be watching on the computer and going, "What's the matter with Jake? He's in forty-second place." My mother is glued to the computer the nine days that I'm racing. But being first into Ophir or something doesn't get me anything. Being first into Nome does.

I wanted to build a team that could win multiple Iditarods, but I was also wondering for a while about how I could spend all of my time training and being away from my family. Every day, year-round. In the 2014 race I was working so hard for a year and then had to scratch and getting no money in return was the icing on the cake. I was pretty banged up. I haven't done anything else for over a decade. I've really been bound by the kennel.

So I sold off my dogs and I am selling my property. I have to get a job, but I haven't decided on a career. I want to have another kid, too. I might be back. It's a possibility. But I definitely wanted a break.

Above Egavik, official Iditarod poster, 2007.

CHAPTER 13

Aaron
BURMEISTER

At thirty-eight, Aaron Burmeister has been around the Iditarod Trail Sled Dog Race his entire life. Raised in Nome, site of the finish line, he could watch the conclusion of the race each year during his formative years. His parents were volunteers and his father, Richard, was a two-time Iditarod competitor when Aaron was a youngster. Richard also wrote a book of poetry about the Iditarod.

Aaron first gave the Iditarod a try in 1994 before completing high school and before attending the University of Alaska Fairbanks. He competed every couple of years for a while before becoming an Iditarod regular in 2003. Burmeister's breakthrough race and best finish was in 2012 when he finished fourth.

Although he studied to become a teacher, the younger Burmeister actually makes his living as the general manager of a business in Nome. Married, Burmeister and wife, Mandy, have two children. In 2009 Burmeister won the Iditarod's Sportsmanship Award and the Spirit of Alaska Award. He also won the Spirit of Alaska Award in 2013.

Despite suffering a knee injury in the early going of the 2014 race, Burmeister turned in one of his finest efforts, leading the Iditarod for a time and finishing seventh. He claimed the first-musher-to-Cripple award of $3,000 in gold.

Being born and raised and growing up in Nome the Iditarod was always very much a part of my life. Both of my parents were very involved. Dad worked as a photographer of the race and my mom was a volunteer coordinating the timing. It's a lifestyle. I was born into a puppy pen, so to speak. Dogs were there and I was raised with them.

Right from the time I was a baby I was with the puppies. I grew up working with the dogs and the pups. It's a lifestyle and a very enjoyable lifestyle. It's a commitment, but it's also something my kids have the opportunity to grow up with and enjoy. From April to November we spend our time in Nome and we spend the winters between Nenana and Fairbanks. We train on the road system now. The dogs are on the road system racing and training.

My father ran the Iditarod in 1979 when I was four years old and I rode the runners to the finish line with him on Front Street. He picked me up at the edge of town and when they were interviewing him on the radio they asked me what my goal was. I said, "When I'm old enough, I want to race." That put my goal and dream into motion, one that I chased for years. As I grew, so did the size of my team. I raced in the Junior Iditarod as a teenager and then as a senior in high school I ran the Iditarod for the first time.

That was a deal that my dad made with me when I was in junior high. I could race the Iditarod when I was eighteen, but then I had to go to college and get a degree before I could come back to it. This means I've been racing since 1994. I can look back at that first race and I can remember every run in it. I can remember every camping spot. I can remember everything. It's strange because the rest of the races seem to blend together.

That rookie race I remember so well and I enjoyed it so much. I took it all in. I had been wanting to do it for so long and I didn't know when I would get back to it again, though I planned to. I finished thirty-seventh in over fourteen days, but that was a monumental moment, an accomplishment, to finish the Iditarod. The 2014 race was my fifteenth Iditarod and most of those others blur together from one year to the next. You pick things out, but I don't remember the details as much as I do from the first race. I can't believe it's my fifteenth Iditarod. I was just sitting down counting them up.

One thing about being from Nome is that you are mushing home and all of the people know you. In that first Iditarod I remember stopping at the top of Cape Nome and going through the team and petting all the dogs because it was almost over. I remember not wanting it to finish. Every year since that race, even now that I'm competing for top places or a fast time, I always stop at the same spot at the crest of Cape Nome. I give the dogs a breather, give them a snack, and kind of reset the race before I make the run into town. That's a very emotional part of the race for me, that last ten miles.

It's going home. You're going to see friends and family. Of course, in 1994, it was a whole life of planning to get to that point, but every race it's a whole year. The whole previous year of training and planning, it's reflecting on the race, what you learned from the race, what you're going to bring to the next one, the training program and the strategy. It's an opportunity to look back at that and that season is just about over when you cross the finish line.

Then you take two days off and you're back at it again. You're already thinking about what you can do better the next year.

Every finish in Nome is kind of exciting. From last year to this year to the year before, every time you cross the finish line, it's an accomplishment. Some years it's just a walk in the park. The years that it was easy, with some of the best finishes, everything went well. Other years were very challenging. Some of the years with the hardest part of racing made it most satisfying to get to the finish. Some of the toughest races were just getting there.

Absolutely, every year is different. You can't predict tomorrow. You can't predict what's going to happen five miles from now, whether it is a moose stepping into the trail or open water on a river. You don't know what you're going to get into. That's the beauty of dog mushing. The beauty of the Iditarod is you can do all of the preparation you want, but you're going to learn something new every day. It might be the certain personality or attitude of a dog, how you're going to feed them, what works, what doesn't. It's a constant challenge and we're always striving to be better at it.

As someone who grew up in Alaska, on the trail essentially, dog mushing was second nature for me. Some mushers grow up in Minnesota and think, *That sounds cool* and they move to Alaska and become Iditarod mushers. If you are growing up with the dogs, you can understand them, you can read them. You know the dogs when they are pups. At the same time, working with the same breed of dogs for years, the same groups of dogs, I can look at a breeding and before the pups are even born I can envision them two years from now. I can even see them going down the trail. I can watch them growing and know certain things I want to train for. I can just tweak them a little bit so that by the time they're two-year-olds or three-year-olds I can fit them in the race team. That's having a history with the breed and the dogs.

When I was a younger musher I thought I knew more than I did. I was talking to my dad a few years ago about when I was twelve years old and taking off out of the kennel with a team of twenty dogs for entertainment. I would run them out of the kennel and go around a loop. There was a highway that ran to Dexter out of Nome and I'd haul the dogs down the highway just to make it more exciting. With twenty dogs I'd ride down out of control for five miles. Today I'm thirty-eight years old and I've been driving dogs my whole life and I'm scared to death to drive twenty dogs like that. I think it's a healthy respect.

You're young and obviously you think you know it all. It takes years to realize that you don't. It takes experience to realize that and now it's the challenge of learning more every day and improving on what you do know. It might be about the sport overall, about the dogs, nutrition, or dog care.

The perfect race can be crossing the finish line—whether you're in first place, thirty-first place, or fiftieth place—and it's so hard to describe it. I've been honored to get the Humanitarian Award and the Sportsmanship Award. I think the time that I might have deserved the Humanitarian Award was when I had to work every stretch of that race to get to that finish line because I had sick dogs. The races that you win an award like that are the races that are a piece of cake. It's the race where everything clicks, there's no extra care, you never have to make the dogs eat and drink the whole way. To call a race the perfect race, you can't really. Who is the most deserving musher?

Somebody who had the opportunity to win the race and represent the Iditarod for a year, that's the opportunity of a lifetime. That's not something you just get. That's something that you earn. Everything falls into place and you have that magic carpet ride. I look forward to someday having that opportunity to win.

It's certainly my goal at this point in my career to win the Iditarod. It's something that I'd be honored to do, to have that opportunity. You work hard for it. You have to earn it, but everything has to fall into place, too.

When I look at the Iditarod I don't see it being much different than it was in the early 1990s or the mid-1990s. Outside, though, over the last twenty years I think the public education of the race has improved. I think a lot of it is due to the Teacher on the Trail program in the schools all over the country. Kids are growing up with so many school districts in different states using it in their curriculums now.

That has certainly improved the education, but you still get the tourists, you still get the people who come to Alaska and everybody's heard of the Iditarod now, but they just don't understand it. So it's a constant, watching the public eye. We're always trying to be role models and educate people, even people here in Alaska.

Alaska still has its own mystique. There is still a romance about Alaska. There is a romance with the Gold Rush and gold mining. Jack London stories brought people up years and years ago. I think the Iditarod is part of that romance and it has the same kind of following.

Being a musher in the Iditarod is more than just being part of a race for ten days or two weeks. That's the part the public follows. Having dogs and a kennel really is a complete lifestyle, not just for you and your immediate family, but for your relatives and everyone who is involved with you. If you called me up and said, "Let's go to dinner next week. Let's sit down and talk," I couldn't commit to the time. That's something that our friends and people we've known for years don't really understand still to this day. You can't commit to anything.

That doesn't affect just me. It affects my family and friends. It's a selfish thing being a musher because if you want to become involved with me, you're in my lifestyle. The kids ought to be helping me build doghouses or help me grooming my trail or training the dogs or traveling to a race. Our lifestyle is so busy and it's all-encompassing. That's something a lot of people just don't understand. It doesn't just affect you, but everyone that's related to you, friends or business associates. Everyone gets drawn into it because that's the lifestyle we have to maintain to race the Iditarod. Certainly you don't get rich racing dogs, but it's a rewarding lifestyle.

There are more things to life than being out on the trail and there are other ways to be part of the Iditarod event than being a participant. I'll always be involved whether I'm on the trail or not. I enjoy being out there. I enjoy the race and the competition. But I enjoy my family, as well. I don't want to sacrifice family to be on the trail.

CHAPTER 14

Cim SMYTH

nother second-generation musher, Cim Smyth, thirty-eight, of Big Lake, has been around sled dogs his entire life. Brother Ramey Smyth is also an Iditarod competitor and his father, Bud Smyth, was an early racer. Smyth grew up in Fairbanks, but he and his wife, Corrine, now live not far from the Iditarod Trail race headquarters.

In his thirteen Iditarod races Smyth has become noted for sometimes racing on foot as fast as his dogs can go with him on the sled. He has had some legendary runs between Safety and Nome, four times covering the last twenty-two miles of the race in the speediest of clockings.

During Smyth's inaugural Iditarod in 1996 when he placed eighteenth, Smyth won the Rookie of the Year Award. He did not return to the Iditarod until 2003, but since then has twice won the Sportsmanship Award and in 2004 was chosen most inspirational musher.

Smyth's best finish is fifth in 2009.

One challenge Smyth must face on the trail that others do not is how to cope with an affliction called Crohn's disease, which is a chronic inflammatory condition affecting the gastrointestinal tract that requires a special diet.

Some symptoms include stomach distress, bleeding, and cramps. The illness resembles colitis.

I grew up with the dogs. I guess when I was eighteen months old I knew all the names of our dogs. That's what my parents tell me. I can't even remember the first time I was on a sled. I don't have any memory of those times because I was so young. That was when I was real little.

When I got a little bigger, five or six years old, I'd be out in the yard when Dad came in from a run. I'd be going, "How'd you do? Who did what?" I'd get the whole blow-by-blow report about each dog and how it was performing. I was really attached to the dogs from the beginning.

It wasn't much of a step from there for me to get involved in running the dogs. We lived rather remotely. It was about three miles at the end of a road and we used the dogs to travel back and forth to the end of the road. We had some more remote land parcels than that and we traveled as much as ninety miles out to those with the dogs. That's how we got around. We gathered firewood, pulled logs, and things like that so by the time I was twelve or thirteen it was something that we did as a job, my chores, and I was excited to go out and do it.

That's how we got work done. That's how we went places. So becoming a musher in those days was under the direct tutelage of my dad. It wasn't as if there was a choice about it. It was something you did unless you wanted to pull a sled behind you. And you didn't. It doesn't take long to learn. If you've got a good dog team it doesn't take long to figure out that mushing dogs is a lot better than walking.

I just always wanted to race. I wanted to run the Junior Iditarod as soon as I heard about it and my brothers and I started training for it. My dad had stopped racing by that time and he let us take the dogs we wanted to use from the kennel. We were all together. Racing was pretty much what we wanted to do and he kind of turned the kennel over to us.

There are ten kids in the family. Most of the other kids weren't as attached to the dogs as my brother Ramey and I. We were more serious about it. My brother Abe, who was a year older than Ramey, trained with us and was pretty heavy into the dogs, but he was never really competitive. He did run the Junior Iditarod and a couple of other little races, but racing never really appealed to him much. For me it did.

When I was in junior high I played soccer and wrestled, but I didn't go to public school much, so I didn't have a chance to play that many sports. I was mostly homeschooled. I definitely had a competitive nature, though. It was mostly a good excuse to drive dogs all of the time. It was like, "I've got to train for the Junior Iditarod. I've got to train for the Iditarod." I was out with the dogs five days a week, all day, or whatever, and I had a good excuse to do it. That was probably what kept me in racing.

I live west of Big Lake in the same area where we were, but there's a road there now so I don't have to use the dogs for transportation to the end of the road. But I use them a lot. I even drive them all the way into Big Lake—it is fourteen miles to town—in the winter whenever I can. I have a car parked there at my folks' place and I'll drive the dogs there and run errands with the car. There's a limited amount you can do in town with a dog team.

I was never pushed to do the Iditarod, but for me it was always a dream of mine to do it. I was probably planning on running the Iditarod before I even knew about the Junior Iditarod. The Iditarod was always out there in front of me. And the idea was exciting for me to think of doing it. To me it was important because I was nineteen [for his first Iditarod in 1996] and I was still with my folks. I was allowed to take all of the good dogs from the kennel. From the beginning it was an exciting adventure for me. I was training on my own. It all felt very important to me. It was a lifelong thing coming to a head, becoming reality.

That year I don't think I was a typical rookie because I wasn't afraid of not being able to do it. I knew I could do it, right from the beginning. But I had an extra interesting little thing thrown in to contend with. I have Crohn's disease and I was in the midst of an attack at the beginning of the race. We hadn't really identified what it was yet, but I was really sick and I was barely able to stand on the sled. But so much had progressed towards doing the race, with the food drops out, everything was ready, that there was no way that I was backing out.

This was pre-diagnosis for me. It was terribly debilitating and it was scary because I didn't know if I was on the road to getting worse. I didn't know what my problem was. All I knew was that I was really, really sick.

I think getting the food drops ready and all of the preparation brought the attack on, but the type of stress I had out there during the race wasn't actually bad for me and I improved as the race went on. When I went out on the trail, for the first few days, all I could do was basically bend over the back of the sled. But about day three I started getting better and by the time I got to Nome, I was fine. It was a big accomplishment for me to get to the end with the illness. I should be in a national commercial for Crohn's disease awareness.

After that I had a hard time getting diagnosed because people didn't believe I had Crohn's disease. They would say, "You couldn't run the Iditarod with Crohn's disease." Yada, yada. It was funny. I have to watch my diet. I'm more careful about it now. It affects what I pack to take on the trail. I just have to pack some medication. That's the regular rule, to make sure I'm not without if something goes wrong. Even with fatigue it's not hard to keep a schedule to take medication. In March you're getting dawn and dark about twelve hours apart. Things are not as hard as they might be in the summer where there is so much daylight or in the middle of the winter where there isn't as much light.

Crossing the finish line in Nome for my first Iditarod was definitely a huge satisfaction. It was a big deal, that first one.

Different things happen in the Iditarod every year. I think one of my most memorable races was in 2004 when I only had five dogs in Nulato. It was my worst finish—forty-third—but it was actually one of my funnest trips. The training hadn't been too good and then my dogs got a little sick just before the race. It turned out they weren't in good enough shape for the race. I thought they were, but with a little sickness about two weeks before the race they were all laid up for a little while. They got out of shape and then we started and all this muscle soreness, little injuries, came up. I just dropped dogs like crazy through the first half of the race.

So I had five dogs left at Nulato with a long way to go in the race, about four hundred miles. That was a challenge. It was tough to face the fact that I couldn't race and that it would be a challenge just to get to Nome. I couldn't drop another dog. I had never experienced that kind of thing. It was the type of thing rookies might face. I never, never thought my dogs would quit. I never had that kind of problem, but when you get down to five dogs [the minimum] and if one tears a toenail off, you're done.

I really had to face the race in a different way and that was definitely a memorable experience. I had a really good time being with those five dogs, trying to strengthen them as I went along so that they would be as invincible as they needed to be to get there. It was different from running a race of attrition where you're just trying to get there as fast as possible. In that case if you have a weak link you just send the dog home. When you're down to five dogs you have to nurse them in a different way. It was extreme coaching, a heightened sense of awareness.

When it's snowing and it's deep and the trail is slow it can be pretty difficult to get along with just five dogs. It snowed several times between Nulato and Nome. Out of Kaltag to get to the first shelter cabin took me a lot longer than it usually does. This was a switch for me. I wasn't able to race down the Bering Sea Coast with only five dogs. That wasn't the goal. The goal was the team at that point. As soon as I became a five-dog musher the goal became the right mix of rest so they would get stronger. I actually smoked on into Nome in an hour and fifty-two minutes from Safety, which is the fastest it's ever been done.

Ramey and I do have a history of covering that part of the trail very fast. I think it's training methods more than anything. I do tend to run a little more than some mushers, but I time my running really carefully. A lot of mushers don't have the sense of timing that Ramey and I were taught, I don't think. We have certain types of timing on our running and I think it shows. We're committed to running all the way on certain stretches so it looks like a lot and has a huge effect when you run all of the way up certain hills rather than trying to run and make it only halfway up every one. I think I have a different style of running and my own physical workouts are of a different style. How I drive my body is a little different than a lot of the others.

I never ran competitively and I don't think I'd be that good at it. I'm fairly good at running in a mushing setting, but long-distance running is totally different. That's an endurance sport for humans. In my case it's sprint after sprint after sprint. You have to run fast for a certain distance and then you're back on the sled and you're freezing your ass off because you're sweating. But you've got to sort of save yourself for the next hill and then sprint on that one. To make the biggest difference, that's how you do it. You sprint the hill and you ride the rest of the time. I'm fairly well suited to that, sprint after sprint. I'm fairly quick, but I might be a little heavy for some sort of long-distance run.

The psychological advantage is big when other mushers know you're coming from behind because they do things they shouldn't. It's always played into both mine and Ramey's advantage, in all races—the little races I've won and the Iditarod—to pick out two or three spots coming into the last checkpoint. A lot of times you're catching people that you wouldn't have caught except they tried to get away when they shouldn't have. They thought they needed some sort of extra boost because you have this reputation of being able to catch them. They try to get away more than they should and their team crashes a little bit. The dogs slow down and they won't respond when they need them to and so you're passing people who have run all out. They made a move a little too early. That's always played into our hands. The psychological factor is big. It definitely has become a trademark.

At times I have had a big rivalry with Ramey, but I don't think it's been huge. It could have been bigger. These days it's more like one guy has a good stretch for a few years and then the other guy has a few good years, so you end up not actually competing head-to-head a lot of the time. If you've got the other guy out there it's because he's falling apart and you're coming on, just in passing. So a rivalry doesn't make much sense. Throughout the sport a rivalry between two people is fairly rare because it's hard for them to stay on the same level and run the same times. There have been a few great rivalries. When we were younger, Ramey and I were racing out of the same kennel and in the beginning years whatever rivalry we had was due to the fact that there was a limited number of resources and we were competing for the resources as well as in the race. There's no off-season trash talking. We get along pretty well. Once we split up and went our own separate ways we had more in common than not in common. Some of it was maturity.

The next goal is to win the Iditarod. I know how it can be done. I've seen a lot, done a lot. I've made a lot of mistakes and learned from them. I have a very realistic outlook on my team compared to what I had in previous years. I can look at my dog team and assess it much more realistically. That's good for me because I've always headed out to win the Iditarod and I crashed it really badly over the years when I didn't have the team to win. I attempted to do it anyway, you know?

Now I make it to the starting line with the best possible team that I've got now. I'll be trying to win, but I'll know if I don't have a chance before the start. A couple of years ago I wouldn't have known. I would have given it a shot to win no matter what, even if I was going to self-destruct along the way. Sometimes everything changes out there. You have to stay close.

Trail of Memories, official Iditarod poster, 2011.

CHAPTER 15

Michelle
PHILLIPS

anadian musher Michelle Phillips from Tagish, Yukon Territory, got her start in long-distance mushing by competing in the one-thousand-mile Yukon Quest. She switched to the Iditarod in 2010 and has competed in five editions of The Last Great Race on Earth.

Although it seems to be an unlikely sporting mix, Phillips's first sports competitions were in figure skating. Members of her family are serious sports fans and competitors and Phillips believes she inherited the fierceness of their will to win.

Operator of Tagish Lake Kennel and its ninety huskies with her partner, Ed Hopkins, also a veteran of the Quest, and her fifteen-year-old son, Keegan, the family provides rides and trips and educational information for tourist visitors. Phillips is known for her cheery personality while racing and in checkpoints. However, one of Phillips's mushing friends, Kelley Griffin, said Phillips has a deceptive killer instinct on the trail despite her friendly exterior.

Phillips was raised in Whitehorse, the capital of the Yukon, but Tagish is more remote, about an hour and a half away in the woods by comparison, a place where cell phone service is much iffier. Rather amusingly, occasionally, there is Internet confusion between musher Michelle Phillips and the one-time singer for the Mamas and the Papas, also named Michelle Phillips.

Between Phillips's stints as a figure skater and her transformation into a dog musher, she was a world traveler, both volunteering to help in needy areas, and determining if she wished to live in another part of the world. Eventually, she chose to return to Canada and eased into a life as a full-time musher.

At forty-six, Phillips has entered six Yukon Quests (owning a top finish of fourth in 2008) in addition to her Iditarods and was given the Vets' Choice Award in the Quest in 2009. After the 2014 Iditarod Phillips was debating if she wished to continue Iditarod racing. At that point her high finish in the Iditarod was sixteenth in 2012, but she also felt she had a higher finish within her and her team.

I skated a lot in Whitehorse and Vancouver, but stopped when I was about sixteen. Figure skating is really hard. I couldn't handle the pressure. I was probably washed up by then. I was having eating disorders. I was a completely different person then. I was wrapped up in outfits [with sequins instead of those rated for forty below].

Afterwards I became somewhat of a world traveler. I did work in mining camps. I usually went to countries that were really different and where people needed help. I was in India, Southeast Asia, Thailand, South America, Ecuador, Colombia, Bolivia, Peru, and Chile. I was looking for a new place to live. I didn't keep too many things. I didn't save many souvenirs. Just a few pieces of art really. Eventually, I realized that the Yukon was a pretty magic place for me. The orphans in Calcutta opened my eyes to the world.

When I got back to Canada I met Ed Hopkins, sixteen years ago. Ed ran in six Quests and I helped him in four of them. I decided when my son was four that I could mush, too. It's kind of a cool thing. I have a very active, competitive family. My mother was a ballerina. My brothers were on the Yukon ski team. My father was a skier.

Mushing was a nice mix. I liked being out in the quiet, in the peace. The dogs are so talented and they give you a lot back. I love being in the wilderness. I love getting up in the morning and training. It definitely is a change of wardrobes switching from figure skating to Carhartts. Yes, my shopping habits, and locations, changed. I do still like getting dressed up for the banquets for the Quest and Iditarod, though.

At the kennel we give tours. We get a lot of cruise ship passengers in the summer. We have a mile loop in the forest for rides. Then we give mushing talks in Carcross.

My first time in the Quest, in a one-thousand-mile race, was 2004. In the beginning it was, "Oh, my God, I'm gonna die." But I was kind of committed. That race I got run over on Eagle Summit by Frank Turner's dog team. He lost his team. I wiped out and got my foot caught between the sleds. I had to crawl out. Frank got the sleds apart. I hurt my left shoulder, too. I couldn't move my arm after that. I couldn't button my coat. I had dislocated my shoulder. It still doesn't work as well as it used to.

Another time in training I wiped out on a corner and after I wiped out again the shoulder hurt. That first Quest, though, after all of that, I came in eighth and I thought, *I did all right.* I was happy. That kept me going. Right away you start to think of ways that you can do better.

You also start to think about how expensive it is to train and to race in the Quest and the Iditarod. All of a sudden I got to thinking, *I have no money. I need to get a job.* Then I was out training in the wilderness, alone, and it was so gorgeous and I thought, *It's sunny. I have my dogs. I have my dog team. It's so beautiful out.* It was one of those epiphanies. *Who cares about a job?* It was a big moment. I knew I wanted to keep mushing.

In 2010 I went over to the Iditarod. I wanted to be part of it. I had to try it. The Iditarod is the top long-distance mushing race in the world. I wanted to see the trail. I wanted to see what it was all about. If you are a long-distance musher you have to enter the Iditarod. But since then I've never felt that I did the best job I could in any race.

The first time I did the Iditarod in 2010 as a rookie I finished twenty-seventh. It wasn't bad, but I had been hoping for more. In 2011 I finished seventeenth. In 2012 I finished sixteenth.

After that race I thought I might be able to make a move in the standings, so in 2013 I expected to be up near the front. I started out that way, but I don't know what it was, with me or the dogs, but I finished twenty-fourth and I just didn't have an explanation of why I didn't do better. I don't know whether I just didn't make the right decisions or not. I hope I can get a higher finish.

Everybody asks about the differences between the Quest and the Iditarod. Some of them are obvious. One big one is that there are more miles between checkpoints in the Quest. There are a lot more things going on in the Iditarod. There are more people on the trail. There are more checkpoints and those checkpoints are villages where people live. You have more wind in the Iditarod. You have to contend with the Bering Sea Coast. There are little nuances that are different.

I don't think I wiped out as much in the Iditarod, well, a couple of times. In the Quest you can see some pretty rough trail, some jumbled ice. In the Iditarod I've been pretty impressed with how well taken care of the trail is. They mark the trail well, especially in those tricky sections like the Dalzell Gorge. There are tons of markers.

In the Iditarod I also feel like they put a lot of effort into the care of the dogs. That's really emphasized. There is a lot more emptiness along the trail in the Quest and I really like going through the village checkpoints in the Iditarod. I really like meeting all of the different people and the elders. One thing about the Quest is that it's pretty lonely.

The first time traveling through the villages in the Iditarod and seeing them and meeting all of the new people, I was really taken with it. After that first Iditarod my first thought was, *I'm coming back.*

Almost as soon as one Iditarod ends I start thinking about what I would do differently on the trail to finish higher. When I finished twenty-seventh in 2010 that's how I was and in 2011 I finished ten places higher. I felt better about my race that year. I felt I could have done better. I always feel that way. I dissect it. It's the whole thing, a combination of things in areas where I think I can improve.

Another great thing in the Iditarod, something I really enjoyed as you mush along, is the changing of the country you go through. The race starts in downtown Anchorage. You go through the Alaska Range. You travel on the Yukon River. And then you switch to the Bering Sea Coast. It makes me feel like I'm really out there in different places.

It's not always fun, though. The Iditarod is demanding and you get tired from so little sleep. I always hit a lull where I start thinking, *This is terrible.* You question yourself and you have to pull yourself out of it. There's always a point on the race when you start thinking that way. You think things are worse than they are. A lot of times it's about the dogs. I go, *Oh, they look terrible.*

They're really tired. I've looked at the dogs that way and it's really me. I saw a picture of me and my team from the Iditarod from a place like that afterwards. I looked at the picture and the dogs looked just great. It was just me.

That's going to happen on a long race when you are pushing yourself. It happens in the middle of the night when it's fifty below zero. It's fatigue.

Going into the 2014 Iditarod I was looking for a good finish. I was thinking I might be taking a break from the Iditarod after that, no more Iditarods for a while, and then go from there to something new. Actually, I want to go back to the Yukon Quest and do it again, maybe in 2015.

CHAPTER 16

Bob
BUNDTZEN

*A*n Anchorage doctor who specializes in infectious diseases, Bob Bundtzen has been an Iditarod regular for twenty years, participating as often as he can in the one-thousand-mile race while periodically skipping a year. Based in Chugiak, Bundtzen grew up in Anderson, Alaska, and attended the University of Alaska Fairbanks and the University of Washington.

Now sixty-five, after entering the 2014 Iditarod, Bundtzen is a veteran of fifteen Iditarods since 1995. The doctor's best finish was twenty-seventh in 1997 and he has also twice finished twenty-eighth. A member of the Chugiak Dog Mushers Association, at times Bundtzen has pooled resources with mushing partner Zack Steer, though Steer is now retired from Iditarod racing.

Over the decades Bundtzen has been involved in numerous other outdoor activities, as well as mushing, including hunting, fishing, and trapping. Although long interested in mushing, Bundtzen did not begin his own Iditarod career until he was in his mid-forties. He was influenced by another older doctor-musher and Iditarod regular—Jim Lanier.

In 1992 I was watching Jim Lanier run and then he hired a good friend and I helped him train quite a bit. I was always interested in dogs. As a kid I had a three-dog team to go trapping in Anderson before it was even named Anderson. So I was always interested in dogs and I started to help Jim a little bit. In the early 1990s I would just take them out to Tudor Track in Anchorage and he was happy to have his dogs run.

Then we started to buy a few dogs together and run them. He had some family problems and I inherited his team. I actually hadn't anticipated or planned to run the Iditarod or race. Jim started encouraging me to run and I said, "Hmm, maybe I'll try it." Up until then my only race was the Chugiak 50, which was two twenty-five-mile heats. My first qualifying race for the Iditarod was the Tustemena 200. I'd never really raced dogs.

I was learning every step of the way. I only had nine dogs and it was a twelve-dog race then. My dogs were all pretty marginal. The Tustemena is a hilly race. I had no idea what I was getting into or how to run it. There were about five of us in the race who had no idea what we were doing.

At the halfway point of the course we got lost. We were way behind. There were four or five others the same as me with their lack of experience, but they all quit. I was last and lost. I was at the back with seven dogs. People know that's a really hard race with only seven dogs. I was pushing that sled up the hills. In retrospect, those dogs had to be in pretty good shape to do that race like that. It was a tough race. I didn't quit.

The next year I did the Knik race and the Klondike and I entered the Iditarod as I had planned. I had a lot of help from people. Jim helped me and one of his friends helped. It was a big step up for me from running three-hundred-milers. I went into the race thinking I would do it once or twice. I did not anticipate doing it over and over again.

I just had the dogs and liked doing it, so I did it. There's a strange attraction. It doesn't attract most people. Once you do the Iditarod it has a hold on you. You always want to do it a little bit better than you did it the last time. It's always wonderful to see the dogs perform well and it's really crummy to see them not run well. When they perform well, there's exhilaration. I finished fortieth in my first Iditarod in 1995.

You read about it and you talk to people, but as a rookie you still don't know what you're in for. As I remember, we had a lot of snow. It was also the coldest race I ever did. It was minus fifty between Kaltag and Unalakleet.

I had good clothing, so mostly I was warm, but where you really get into trouble is when you have to take your gloves off to do something with the dogs. I had big beaver mitts and I had heaters in the mitts. When I had to do chores I'd put them right back on to warm up my hands. Then you do the next thing. Everything slows down tremendously.

In retrospect I'm really surprised and amazed that the dogs didn't get injured because I was really inexperienced. I thought, *Oh, these dogs, they do well no matter what the temperature is.* But as the years have gone on I have had some trouble with frostbitten dogs. That time the dogs came out of it just fine. No injuries. I did the same. I didn't injure anything. No frozen toes or fingers.

The whole race was extremely cold. The Yukon River was really cold, always minus thirty to minus forty. It was a good trail, too, because there hadn't been any snow for a long time. It was just packed, which helped out a lot. When it's that cold, you're just careful. Somehow I made it just fine. It took me fourteen days. I went really slow. That didn't used to be slow, but the race has speeded up.

It felt pretty fantastic to be there in Nome after you've been out there for fourteen days and done all that. To think that you were able to come through it without any difficulty was great. My son Travis was under the arch. He was twelve then. And my wife, Joan, and friends were there to greet me, so it was really something. I think I was the last musher to finish before a storm came in and we didn't see another musher for two days. I was lucky there. At that point I figured I was going to do it again.

I didn't anticipate doing the Iditarod this long. The last couple of years [2011 and 2013], I had leader trouble and didn't finish. Those leaders are gone. I sold them. I always have trouble on the Bering Sea Coast.

There is a lot of interest in the Iditarod, but I don't travel Outside much. But when I was governor of the Alaska Chapter of the American College of Physicians Internal Medicine, I was traveling Outside for five years. Once they found out I was an Iditarod musher they became very interested.

They were saying, "What's it like out there?" Most of those folks live in cities. They really have no concept of anything like this. They go to national parks and they have trails, or they're paved. They really have no concept of wilderness. They ask, "How can you stand it away from people?" Or, "Aren't you frightened out there?"

Zack Steer and I have had a kind of unofficial partnership. We shared dogs and a few years we would actually run two teams. He'd run the best team and I'd take the rest of the dogs and run them slower. I just liked working with them.

Zack was winding down because he was selling the Sheep Mountain Lodge and moving because his kids were starting school. He couldn't have dogs where he was moving. And I'm not a full-time musher. I'm a doctor. I have a pretty full life. Every weekend is spent with dogs. I have help and they run the dogs when I'm not running them. The miles on the dogs aren't what they are on some of the other teams. I know exactly where I want to be mileage-wise and I do a lot of the qualifying races. They're fun to do. You compare yourself to other people and it requires a huge commitment.

I have twenty or so dogs, all of the competitive ones. I am one of the last mushers from Anchorage. There have been big changes, but there are more kennels than you might think in Anchorage, but they're small, recreational kennels and might be sprint teams. All of the big teams have moved out. There are several in the Chugiak-Eagle River area, but most of the mushers have moved farther away from the city. All the professional mushers have moved out. Hopefully I will do this a little bit longer, but I'm too old to breed dogs. It takes three or four years before you have a competitive dog team and I don't anticipate doing it too much longer. I'll be too old. I thought 2014 might be my last Iditarod, but I've said that before.

As everyone says, every Iditarod is different. I've had a couple of episodes where I got stranded on top of Rainy Pass. Once, I got stuck in a bad windstorm with a young team and I didn't have a leader that would lead me over. I had a new harness setup and I could not haul them over, so I ended up stopping and waiting for the next day. It was blowing hard. I was there about twelve hours and the wind was blowing and it was chilly. Everybody came out of it fine. I didn't freeze anything. You just take care of the dogs, feed them a couple of times, and just kind of huddle down and try to sleep for a little bit.

Some of the most fantastic times I've had on the Iditarod Trail were traveling up the Yukon River in clear weather with the northern lights out. That's just some of the most fantastic experiences. Back in the nineties when the Hale-Bopp Comet was out, some of those nights were beautiful. Mushing along with the northern lights out and the comet there, those are some of my nicest memories. One of the other things that happens out there when you're mushing along usually occurs when there hasn't been a lot of wind and the trees are heavily laden with snow and you're really tired. You're just kind of falling asleep and you watch these trees as you go by and you see shapes of goblins and people and things on the snow in the trees. It's just amazing. You can call them hallucinations. They look just like people.

As a doctor what I do is internal medicine and most of what I do is infectious disease consultation. Usually by the time I have seen a patient more than once they know I'm a musher. They ask me about it all the time and encourage me. Whenever I say, "I'm going to do the Iditarod this year" they all say, "Oh, good" and they kind of jump up and down. There are a lot of folks who follow me in the Iditarod when I run it who don't usually follow it. Just people I work with. That's kind of my fan club.

I think the Iditarod is the most unifying thing in Alaska, but I don't get a lot of mail about it. Mostly, it's one-on-one and asking me if I'm running it that year. In the big picture, it's all been fun. It's also a lot of work, a tremendous amount of work. But you know, most things in life that are worth doing are actually a lot of work. Since I don't win any money, I guess it's a hobby. It's something I really like to do. You have to feed the dogs every day and scratch their ears, and of course there's training.

To be honest, it's extremely expensive. You see so many really good up-and-coming mushers who would make the sport better, but they just have to stop because they can't afford it. I think people in general, but especially businesses, really need to support individual mushers. They need to support them if they want to keep the quality of the race up. That's one thing that disappoints me. I think a lot of people benefit from the Iditarod who do not support individual mushers. People need to help them out. It's probably more difficult over the last couple of years because of the economy. People don't realize how much money, time, and effort it takes for a musher who doesn't have a big sponsor to get there. It's difficult. Even if you're winning, it's difficult.

If you look at the other competitive sports out there, we're pretty small, dollar-wise. National outdoor outfitters are good, but I think some of our local businesses should support the mushers more. Alaska businesses. There are a lot of hotels here and I don't know if they support the mushers. They benefit significantly. I think the Iditarod is something that all the communities need to support strongly.

The dogs don't surprise me as athletes now because I know what they're capable of, but if you look at some of the studies that are done, it's astounding what they do. From a physiological standpoint, these dogs are unique to any other animal in the world really. I don't know how they do it, or why they do it, but they do it. Mike Davis, a veterinarian, did these studies at the University of Oklahoma.

You're out there in the race and you're tired and you know the dogs have to be tired and they just keep going and going and going and you start scratching your head and say, "Why are they doing this?" And other people are saying, "Why are they doing this?" It's amazing because when you stop they start jumping up and down in harness, jerking, because they're ready to go. They want to go. It's crazy. The best dogs are still jumping up and down at the finish line in Nome. But it's what they want to do.

Some of my best races, for a total race, were the second and third ones when I was twenty-seventh and twenty-eighth. Everything just went well. I had pretty much all my own dogs and I had trained them. Nobody was injured and I finished with big teams, thirteen dogs, and it just feels good when that happens. My last couple of races [2011 and 2013] I was actually doing much better, but I had to scratch on the Coast because of my leaders. I still had a functional team, but I didn't have a leader that wanted to go. I had dogs that were jumping up ready to go, but the leaders are key, of course.

My goal each year is not a number, but just to do the best we can. I do as well as I can with the dogs I've got and as the years have gone on we have gotten better and better dogs. Some people can run dogs better than others. There are more mushers than ever at the top who are contenders. Makes it more exciting that way, doesn't it? If I can make the top twenty I'd be doing pretty good. Those couple of years when I scratched on the Coast, I think I would have if I had a leader that would have kept going. I'm sure that I've run teams that were top ten, but I just can't run them that well.

I do think the Iditarod is the most unifying thing for the state and it's probably the one thing people think about when they think about Alaska now elsewhere. Even worldwide, not just in the United States.

Sweet Dreams, print, 2004.

CHAPTER 17

Joanne
POTTS

One of the mainstays of Iditarod administration for years, Joanne Potts has been involved with the race behind the scenes for nearly forty years. A member of the *Anchorage Daily News's* Iditarod Hall of Fame, Potts has filled several key roles since starting out as a volunteer in the mid-1970s.

Potts, seventy-four, and her family moved to the Anchorage area in 1975 and she started working as an Iditarod volunteer in 1976. She has been a staff member since 1982. Potts has held various titles, including race director and race coordinator, but some mushers refer to Potts as "Superwoman" for all of the time and effort she puts into the race. Potts and Art, her husband of a half century, are originally from Kentucky.

I was living in Eagle River in 1975 and met a woman who had kids the same age and when it was getting on towards winter and I wasn't working she asked me, "How would you like to volunteer for the Iditarod?" I said, "What's the Iditarod?" I had just moved to Alaska and I didn't know. Actually we had lived in Southeast Alaska for five years. She explained it to me and said she volunteered and would give me something to do.

It sounded like fun. At that time Anchorage Iditarod headquarters was at the old Hilton Hotel. It was a tiny little room. There weren't many of us that did shifts there and I volunteered for two hours a night on Wednesdays and Fridays for two weeks.

That meant I was answering the telephone and answering questions. We had a recorder and put messages on them and played them so people could get recorded updates about the race. We put information about the top ten mushers on there. If that's all you wanted you could get that on a recording. But if you wanted to talk to somebody you had to call another number. They asked where "John Jones" was. I met some of the Iditarod people and the next year they asked me to open a headquarters in Eagle River because so many mushers lived there. For two years I ran an Iditarod headquarters in the back of a drugstore in Eagle River. They just had a little space. I had a blackboard and a table there during the race.

I only did that during the race so people didn't have to go into Anchorage to find things out. They could come see the board in Eagle River and see where the mushers were in the standings and to get information. It was just more convenient for them. I also worked in a booth at the state fair in the summer, too, selling merchandise. Then I went back into Anchorage and ran the headquarters there during the race.

Other than the Iditarod I also worked as a substitute teacher at Service High School, usually as a long-term sub for teachers who were pregnant and on maternity leave. I remember I had [current musher] Jim Lanier's daughter in my class. But I told them I couldn't do it in March because I was volunteering for the Iditarod. We had the headquarters at the Sheraton for two years and I was in charge of getting the volunteers and setting up their schedules at the headquarters. I believe that was in 1979 and 1980 and then we went back to the Hilton. In the summer of 1982 I became race coordinator.

It was in 1982 that my family moved to Wasilla and that year the Iditarod moved to Wasilla and I started working in the headquarters, staffing the office, as a volunteer. I had quit my subbing in Anchorage when we moved to Wasilla and I didn't have a job so I said, "Sure, but I'm not going to work past June because my kids will be out of school and we have a new place here. I want to have time to get flower beds going." They said, "OK, we'll have somebody hired for this job by then." Well, they didn't. They didn't get anybody hired. They didn't try very hard to hire anybody. Lois Harter and I shared the office for a summer and we shared a $600 salary.

That office was above Teeland's store in Wasilla. Then at an Iditarod board meeting my name was brought up for the job to then-president Bob Sept. I tell this story not to badmouth Joe Redington because I love Joe dearly, but he did not want me to get the job. He had walked in on me at Teeland's one day and it was a blistering hot day there. No one else was there and there was nothing to do and I had my feet up on the desk. Joe walked in and he was upset because I was sitting there with my feet on the desk. He just thought that was the tackiest thing he ever saw in his life. He goes, "You know, you're working for the Iditarod, blah, blah, blah." Joe kept saying, "She can't do this. You've got to give this job to someone classier than she is. She had her feet up on the desk when I went in." That became the issue. But I got the job.

I got the job in August and in September they said I had to go to Nome. I had only been to Nome once as a friend of a musher. But this time I was going because of things that had happened in the 1982 race. Howard Farley and his wife, Julie, were handling the headquarters there. But Iditarod people in Wasilla sent someone to take over and they sent someone to take over the merchandise sales and somebody else to handle the dog lot. The people in Nome were hostile to what was going on. My orders were to go to Nome and make everybody happy. And after all of that stink about me having my feet on the desk and not wanting me to get the job, Joe Redington came up to me at the state fair booth and said, "You're a good one to do this. Do it right."

So I was sent to Nome. I didn't know anybody up there besides Leo Rasmussen and Dick Gallagher, who were both on the board of directors. I was told to contact Rosemary Phillips [who later became executive director of the Iditarod] because she had a big house and I could probably stay with her. I contacted her when I got there and she said she had a house full of miners and I would have to stay in a hotel the first night and then she would introduce me to all these people. I didn't know Rosemary from Adam at the time. The first day I went out around Nome by myself. There was a place that eventually became Fat Freddie's restaurant that had a turn-of-the-century-type Gold Rush show where the women dressed up and were dancing. It was pretty cool.

I was by myself and this guy came up to me and introduced himself and asked what I was doing there. I told him I was with the Iditarod and he said, "Then you're in trouble." Like I was the enemy or something. I went, *Uh, oh, oh my God, what am I doing here?* We became good friends later, but I told Lois about it the next day on the phone and she said that guy wasn't too happy with the Iditarod. She gave me advice. She said, "You need to talk to everybody and you need to promise that we will not try to control what goes on in Nome. What you need to do is find somebody who will be coordinator of the activities in Nome and appoint people to do things and tell them you will be a resource." Well, I did that. I spent three days going around to see everybody and anybody in Nome and promising that and I got a Nome coordinator: Rosemary started to do it.

Meanwhile, while I was in Nome Jack Frost quit as executive director. He was gone. It wasn't like two weeks' notice. Joe started making noise right away about making Rosemary executive director and I said, "You can't make her the executive director, she's going to be Nome coordinator." But she ended up getting the job as executive director. I had to go back to Nome and find somebody to be Nome coordinator and that's when I latched onto Paul Sterling. He was wonderful. Everybody just loved Paul and so if Paul asked them to do anything, they'd do it.

The Iditarod is much bigger now than it was, but at that time, after I got hired, the only other people in the office were Greg Bill and Rosemary and two girls that shared the office manager job. That was it. Those two girls weren't there at the same time. I was race coordinator and I held that title for several years.

I never dreamed I would be working for the Iditarod for so many years. I thought I was going to go back to teaching in the Mat-Su Valley. When you're teaching school, and I love teaching school, you see 120 kids a day. It's the same 120 people every day for ten months. The thing that really captured me when I first started working for the Iditarod was the people I talked to from all over the world. It floored me. I remember the guy from London named Ian Woodridge who wrote for the *London Times* who coined the phrase "The Last Great Race on Earth." The board, or Rosemary, I can't remember, wanted to make it our mantra and I had to call him for permission. He was very, very British. It was hard to understand his accent. He said he would send us something that said we could use it and we could get it copyrighted and it could be our thing. He didn't care.

One time I talked to the rest-of-the-story guy, Paul Harvey. They cancelled the Fur Rendezvous for lack of snow and it came out as the big race in Alaska was cancelled and he said on his show that the Iditarod was cancelled. We got calls right away from one of the English guys, Allen Cheshire, who was signed up. His sponsors had heard it on Paul Harvey and we hadn't heard it yet. Allen said we had to do something quick because he was going to lose all his sponsors. I had to call Paul Harvey's show and I talked to a woman and said, "We need to correct something that was on his show." She said, "Just a minute" and the next thing I knew Paul Harvey was on the phone. Afterwards I thought, *My God, I just talked to Paul Harvey.*

It has been fun and even from my home state of Kentucky there are a lot of people that are connected to the Iditarod. You hear a voice that sounds like Kentucky and you say something and it turns out they lived twenty miles from your hometown. We went back to Kentucky for our fiftieth wedding anniversary and fiftieth high school reunion. After the reunion a couple I met in Alaska had a party at a hotel in Lexington and I brought a friend who had nothing to do with Alaska to the reunion. She said, "Who are all of these people?" I said, "Well, gee whiz, I've met all of these people through the Iditarod."

My family got to know the mushers just as everyday people. My kids always took it for granted. My daughter Valerie met a gal who was a Susan Butcher fan in Lexington, Kentucky, and she didn't understand how someone could be a fan of an athlete or a celebrity. Once this girl found out Valerie knew Susan Butcher she was constantly badgering her to get Susan Butcher's autograph. She got some stuff together and sent them for Susan to sign. We were back and forth for two years with stuff for Susan to send to this girl. Valerie just thought it was the stupidest thing she ever heard of because she grew up around all of the mushers and they were just people to her.

Sometimes when you sit back and think about it you get reminded how huge a thing the Iditarod is. I was raised in Richmond, Kentucky, and they think it's a pretty amazing thing that this hometown girl is involved in something as big and important and well known as the Iditarod. For the most part I guess I take it for granted because I work with the mushers all of the time and I work with them very well. I'm really their primary contact. I feel like they're my kids. I feel like I take care of them. John Baker always says I have to take care of him because he's from the Bush. That's because the first year he ran he didn't know how to fill out the paperwork and I helped him.

I answer all of the mushers' questions, their smart questions and their dumb questions. Rookies—and sometimes even those that aren't rookies—need a little handholding sometimes. I always try to answer their questions and I always try to be prompt in getting back to them. I don't put people off. I try to get back to them as quickly as possible and they know it and appreciate it. I always feel they appreciate me.

When I was chosen for the Iditarod Hall of Fame in 2013, Beth Bragg, the *Daily News* sports editor, was the one who told me. She came over to the Millennium Hotel headquarters and it was the busiest day of our year, before the banquet and she said she had to talk to me. She told me and it actually took my breath away. It was just so startling. For a minute I couldn't even believe it. Oh, gosh, was I surprised. I had never dreamed of that. The more I thought of it, it was so humbling to think that I got votes for that. And then they announced it on the public address system at the beginning of the race.

Everyone was coming up to me saying, "Oh, congratulations. You deserve it. If anybody does, you deserve it." I was humbled and very proud of getting that. It's not something that I would have ever set my cap to because I know mushers who are not in there, not little old Joanne Potts. That's how it felt to me. It was pretty exciting. They had taken my picture without telling me why—they didn't want it made public yet. We were doing food drops and the photographer asked me to stand up. I was eating and I didn't want to do it. I thought, *How stupid is this? You're supposed to be taking pictures of what's going on and you want me to stand up for a picture?* Then I saw the paper and that was the picture he took at the food drops. I figured that one out afterwards. It definitely caught me off guard and there aren't too many things in my life that have caught me off guard.

I don't think I have a favorite Iditarod because for me what happens is that when the next one comes around the others go to the back burner and this one becomes important. People also ask me if I have favorite musher. I think about people like Lance Mackey whom I've known since he was seven years old. I really feel attached to the ones I've known since they were kids. But when Dallas Seavey comes across the finish line first I get just as much of a thrill because I've worked with these guys all season long and I get to really know them. So I don't really single them out.

One Iditarod that was among the most memorable was the 1991 race when we had the actor Hugh O'Brian come to Nome to give out a Wyatt Earp replica pistol. That year Rick Swenson won his fifth championship and we had all kinds of storms. I was stuck in Kotzebue. The plane was supposed to land in Nome and we couldn't because of the snow. Everybody is trying to get to the finish line. There were twenty-six of us. Kotzebue was in a horrible, horrible snowstorm and Nome was clear, but we couldn't get there. We listened to the finish on the radio at the Kotzebue airport.

Then Alaska Airlines, which is a race sponsor, told us they had a plane coming to pick us up and it was a freighter and they were just going to use it for passengers. Everyone was out there with snow shovels and heavy equipment to make sure that plane got in. I missed Rick Swenson, but I walked in just as Martin Buser [who finished in second place three hours later] was coming down the chute.

There was also the time I got stopped for having a gun on an airplane. It was probably 1988. We had allowed Alaska Continental Bank to make a gun that had an Iditarod connection that they gave away if you put enough money in a certificate of deposit. Then they went belly up. I don't know what happens to stuff when companies go bankrupt, but they went in and they found five of these guns and because it said Iditarod they assumed they belonged to us.

One of them became a raffle prize. I was given the gun along with a solid gold Iditarod belt buckle. It was wrapped up and it said on top, "Deliver to Rosemary Phillips in Nome." When I was handed the box I was told, "Do not let this out of your sight. This box is worth over $5,000." So I took that seriously and I watched over the box. It was carry-on.

I left the hotel the next morning to make a six o'clock flight to Nome. I was with the guys from Iams dog food. I took my bags through the check-in line and waited and waited and waited and my bags didn't come back. Pretty soon I noticed everyone was going over to the next line. Tom Fletcher and I were the only ones left. Tom got his bag. Pretty soon here comes this little security guy carrying my bag and the minute I saw him, I knew. I said, "Oh, my God, Tom, there's a goddamn gun in that bag."

I said to the security guard, "Yeah, that's my bag" and he said, "Will you come with me?" He walked me over to the corner and called for assistance. Four more security people came from someplace. It took five security people to walk me through the airport and down the steps at the Anchorage airport. I had my head down. I didn't want anybody to see me with the security guys. I passed Dean Osmar's wife.

They took me to a room and they opened the box. Then one of them goes, "M'am, you know this is worth ten years in jail or a $10,000 fine." Then I fell apart.

Of course I missed the plane. Tom Fletcher got to Nome and told Rosemary Phillips what happened and she called. She wanted to know if she should call the Iditarod attorney. But when they said ten years or $10,000 I just lost it. We called Bill MacKay, who was vice president of Alaska Airlines, and always a big supporter. The security guard goes, "Mr. MacKay, this is John, your friendly security guard, at the airport. I just want to tell you that we just took a gun away from a passenger who was going to carry it on the airplane and she would like to talk to you. Her name is Mrs. Potts." I was crying so hard I couldn't talk to Bill and he said, "What's going on? What's wrong?" He said, "Never mind, I'll be right over there," and in less than five minutes he walked through that door.

Bill came in and wrapped me in a big old bear hug and said, "Don't worry." Security had already called the FAA and the FBI. The FAA had come and taken pictures of me with the gun. Bill called the FBI and said they didn't need to come. He explained it to them. Bill got the box and there were a lot of raffle tickets in there, too, which I didn't know. And those idiot security guys wanted to buy raffle tickets on the gun. So I'm sitting there and they're buying $25 raffle tickets and hoping to hell none of them won because I was mad as hell.

Bill took me to the Alaska Airlines Board Room and told them I was his guest until they could get me on the next plane to Nome. I had a bagel and cream cheese and a Bloody Mary. We had projected that Susan Butcher was going to come in and win in the afternoon and I asked if we could put on whatever channel was covering the Iditarod and they did and there was Susan in the damned chute and I missed it sitting in the airport in Anchorage.

How they worked it out after that was that Bill gave the gun to the pilot and when we got to Nome the pilot gave it to me when I got off the plane. By the time I got to Nome everybody knew about it. People kind of shied away from me, didn't want to get close to me because "You're a criminal." And someone said, "Here comes Joannie get your gun!" Actually, I had some kind of post-traumatic stress from it and I couldn't deal with the teasing.

That night there was a shindig at the recreation center with Marge Ford and the Polka Chips and I couldn't have a good time. I was crying. I told Rosemary I was going to go home the next day because I wasn't doing anybody any good. I called my husband, Art, and he's a mental health professional. He said, "Well, just sleep on it and see how you feel in the morning." The next morning I did feel completely different and when they teased me I could come right back at them. Rich Owen said I should write a book about my memorable experience and I said, "I don't think my grandchildren need to hear about this."

At the moment my title is assistant race director of the Iditarod. I was born in 1940, but I don't feel old. I don't feel any different than I did ten years ago. As long as I'm doing my job and getting it done OK, I don't feel like retiring.

CHAPTER 18

Mark
NORDMAN

One way or another Mark Nordman, sixty, has been involved with the Iditarod Trail Sled Dog Race since 1983 when he first competed. Nordman raced in five Iditarods in the 1980s and 1990s while being based in Grand Marais, Minnesota. Nordman first became interested in mushing in the 1970s while living in northern Minnesota. His race finishes were in the thirties and forties.

However, after Nordman stopped competing in the Iditarod he stayed connected as a race official, eventually progressing to race marshal, the chief judge on the trail. His technical title is director of race logistics and competition, but while that may be how it appears on paper no one addresses him as such. Once the race begins Nordman's law is the law of the trail. If a musher runs into trouble it is Nordman who makes the decision about whether or not he should be penalized and how much of a penalty will be suffered, or if a musher is injured, whether or not he must withdraw from the race.

Nordman oversees rules enforcement and makes the tough judgment calls that govern the lives of mushers and dogs during the race, frequently flying back and forth along the one-thousand-mile trail to consult with other officials, judges, and checkers on matters of import as the teams speed toward Nome.

He is also the ambassador to the villages located along the trail, the point man who consults with locals and works to make sure they know they are appreciated even though rules changes implemented over the years in the interest of competitive fairness prevent mushers from going to private homes to eat and rest.

Before he became enamored of dog mushing and moved to Alaska, Nordman was enthralled by hockey and as a young man was a goalie at the University of Minnesota.

I stumbled across a sled-dog race in the early seventies in Minnesota and took an interest in it. I always had a big interest in Canada and the north. I'd done a bunch of traveling and I had met some guys who had been working on the first Iditarod in 1973. Phil Fleming was a checker out of Salmon River. I heard about the Iditarod from guys who had come back to Minnesota after working on building the Alaska Pipeline. I met them and I met my mushing mentor, Tim White, the famous sled builder. I was living in Duluth. That was before I moved to Grand Marais, where I lived for twenty years.

In 1976 I went to Alaska with Tim to run the Knik 120. I was just helping him and then I spent some time in the Northwest Territories and enjoyed it. I ran my first Iditarod in 1983 and I was a judge in 1988. I competed in five Iditarods and finished four.

My whole reason for wanting to run the Iditarod was to see the state, to see the people, and travel across Alaska. I'm not a competitive person at heart although I've done well in some shorter races. About twelve years ago I moved to Alaska and it became home. For years I was coming up to Alaska every three or four months for meetings or purchasing dogs or visiting people.

It's been a great ride. The Iditarod opened a lot of avenues to me also. As race marshal I've been able to go to races worldwide. I've spent four or five summers in Argentina running dogs and helping to put on races there. I flew my own dogs from northern Minnesota to Buenos Aires and to Ushuaia, the capital of Tierra del Fuego. That is about ninety miles from Cape Horn and it's the southernmost city in the world. I was able to work races in Spain, in Europe, and all over Canada. It's pretty much what I enjoy doing and it's a passion. It's been great. The 2014 race was my twentieth year as race marshal. Time really does fly.

I always played a lot of hockey. I definitely enjoyed athletics, mostly hockey, and I thought I would end up in athletic administration. I was interested in working with adaptive physical education classes. I was a union steward on a big construction job on the north shore of Lake Superior. It was somewhat like the Iditarod. There were like six hundred or seven hundred guys who did business with the union, with occasional conflict and a lot of emotions.

My first Iditarod was 1983. My wife at the time and I came to Fairbanks and stayed with a friend there. We did food drops, which for any rookie is probably the biggest nightmare around. I did everything ass backwards from the start. I cut up the meat in perfect little pieces for all the early checkpoints and by the time we got close to the end everything was frozen in big blocks because we ran out of time before we had to ship it out.

It was a different time in the race. At that time you could still stay in people's homes in the villages and that was a huge benefit to the community. Since we are no longer doing that in my position over the last ten years I've been trying to get the communities to stay more involved with us. Don't just bring a meal to Mark Nordman, bring a meal to all of the mushers. I'm trying to get the communities back into it and I think we're doing a lot better on that.

That change was a big dividing line in the race. From the standpoint of competition it was a good thing to level the playing field, but without rural Alaska, without these villages, we don't have an Iditarod.

In 1983 I was nervous and excited about doing the race. It was the first year that we started in downtown Anchorage. I overslept on the way to the starting line. I had the rookie panic of buying everything at the last minute that I might need and I was sharpening my axe at the last minute. Then by the time you reach Rainy Pass you realize you didn't really need all that stuff and you might as well send it home.

I had a nice dog team. It was a good, experienced bunch of dogs I had collected from veteran mushers. The race was an emotional roller coaster. I don't think it's as physically demanding as many of us have said before. It's mental trying to get used to the lack of sleep. That's why truck drivers and physicians and those who don't have an eight-to-four job who don't need to have eight hours sleep, succeed. It was all new to me going through Nikolai. Before that I had never been off the road system in Alaska. It was a cold race at that point. I met a lot of people in that first year who are now very dear friends of thirty years.

Tears are coming down your face when you finish—I heard this a lot from mushers—and you don't know whether you want it to be over and you don't know if you're crying because you're glad you finished or because it's over. For the first few days after you finish you go around thinking, *Boy, I'm glad I got that done.* Back in Minnesota I was sleeping on the floor because you can't get used to sleeping on a bed and then you're already making plans for the future to do it again.

My favorite race was the first one. It was the people, the newness of doing it, the ups and downs. I thought, *Is this ever going to end?* But then when I got to the end I didn't want it to end.

In 1988 I leased my team to a physician named Bill Gallea, so I didn't have a team. I had done some race officiating in Minnesota and I had the opportunity to come to Alaska and be an Iditarod race judge. Then in 1989 I got asked to be race marshal. That first year I was a judge around Shaktoolik. Being a dog musher you end up working for the competitors, of course within the rules. But you're kind of the go-to guy, so just like racing you don't get much sleep trying to make sure everybody is happy, the dogs are happy, and the villagers have good interaction with us.

A lot of people come to you with questions. It's been set up that way and to this day you're the person who is the liaison between the communities, the checkers [hopefully local checkers], volunteers, and the veterinarians who come in. Everything kind of filters through that judge. Then the judges report to the race marshal. The race marshal kind of oversees all things once the event starts. The first year I did it in 1989 it was pretty intimidating. The mushers were my peers. You sit in meetings with all of these mushers you've looked up to like Rick Swenson and Susan Butcher and Jerry Austin. So it was interesting that first year, but I liked it.

I'm someone who really doesn't like conflict and so it's a strange position to have for one who doesn't like conflict. As a side note, the first year I was race marshal I got around a dozen Christmas cards. The next year I got one and I continue to get one. I've had tough decisions to make and lots of dealings with good people.

My role in Iditarod is probably the most heartfelt thing I've ever dealt with. Richard Strick Jr., a volunteer, went up into Rainy Pass on a snowmachine to smooth the trail and was buried in an avalanche in 2006. He lost his life there. When Jerry Austin died I went to the memorial there in St. Michael. It's hard to see good people that were important to this event pass away.

I think I've gained respect from the mushers because I've been there. I've won a couple of races—definitely not the Iditarod. I've finished in the back of the pack. I've scratched in some races. I feel pretty comfortable with the sport. After my first time as a race marshal I went back to racing the Iditarod for a few years before I became race marshal again. I've been involved with the sport for a long time. I look at their equipment. I look at the food drops and try to keep up with what a new generation of mushers is doing. I interact with these people and I get to know them really well. I can tell if Musher A is upset with Musher B, even if it has nothing to do with the race. Maybe there was a bad dog deal. Maybe something happened outside of the race is something you see.

It's a little bit like becoming the coach of a team that you played on. I was a teammate and now I'm the boss. I think I can have a good relationship with all these people, have dinner with the family when I travel throughout the state. Yet I've had to make some really hard calls on people that affected their lives hugely. That's really tough.

One thing I do like about this sport is that every year is a new year. You sign up for the Iditarod each year and it's a new slate. It doesn't matter what happened in the past. You have to keep your mind on that. It may be a fact that someone had a tough run a few years ago, but it doesn't exist. That's the type of thinking you have to attain.

Everybody gets to Nome under the rules. My goal, and sometimes I've been criticized for it in the past, though not in recent years, is that maybe I'm too easygoing. It's a big deal to run the Iditarod. You, me, could not run the Indianapolis 500 next year no matter what. There's no way it would happen. I don't care how much money you had, it couldn't happen. This event allows people that have a passion for dogs to travel across the wilderness to do the Iditarod. Yes, we have qualifying races, but if you put your heart and mind to it, you can make it happen. I don't want to have somebody not make it to Nome for a little reason, for a small misunderstanding. You still have to follow the rules, for sure, but there's judgment. That's what it is. I know some people say that things need to be black and white. I've never understood how things can be so black and white when you're talking about being a judge. Otherwise, why have a judge?

The Iditarod is better known in the Lower 48 than it ever was. I say that as someone who lived in the Lower 48 for a long time. But social media is really what has changed everything as far as promotion of the event goes. It's an interesting deal where you start hearing stories about specific dogs, or the players. There's always been interest in the dogs, but I think there's more. Right now Alaska is a hot potato. Everybody wants to know more about Alaska. You've got every kind of reality show out there imaginable.

It is incredible how many there are. I shake my head at most of them. But people hear about Alaska and they want to pick up on it. The race has gotten faster, of course. My first race took eighteen days. My last finish was thirteen days. Now so many mushers finish in nine days. You're always improving. Everybody wants faster sleds, wants to figure out a way to get the dogs more rest, and the mushers are trying to figure out how to get more rest. Very few people can keep up with these huskies. The human is the weak link.

Every musher wants to improve. The people in the checkpoints want to improve. They want to make sure their checkpoint is the best, which may mean being quicker fixing hot water for feeding of the dogs. Our trailbreakers take a lot of pride in what they do. We've got eight snowmachines that go out in front of the mushers. We've got trail sweeps that go behind them. We groom some of the trails. People say, "Oh, you're making it too easy." But you're still going across Alaska. You're still going over the Alaska Range. It can't be too easy. Maybe you're making a trade-off. Maybe the trail is a little better than it was, but you're going so much faster. It's harder on the mushers for sleep deprivation.

The weather is absolutely an element. You have champions that get stuck in checkpoints. You wouldn't expect that after all these years. But it happens. Routinely we have strong winds on the Yukon River or on the Bering Sea Coast. A couple of years ago we had it both places. You just never know.

Interest has increased with the average person in the Lower 48. The amount of traveling I do, I might be sitting on an airplane and be asked, "What do you do?" I tell them and they say, "Oh, I've heard about that." They also say, "Isn't that the race that woman won?" They're talking about Susan Butcher, not Libby Riddles. Isn't that incredible? You still hear that so many years later.

In the office at Iditarod headquarters the tour buses just keep rolling in. I was just in Nome for five days. We were working on taking care of the finish-line arch. But in a short period of time we had three parties come up and want to have their pictures taken underneath the arch even though it was not in the street, but in the old public works building with scaffolding all around it and I was staining it.

The Iditarod is pretty well known internationally. It really is a dream for people to do it. The Iditarod has spun off a lot of races internationally. It definitely still surprises me how the Iditarod is such a unifying thing statewide. People are calling the mushers by their first names, "DeeDee [Jonrowe]," "Martin [Buser]," and "Jeff [King]." It's like with Brazilian soccer players—"Pele."

When you do something every day, which I do with my Iditarod work, you know it's special, but you don't always remember what a unique Alaskan event it is. You can sit down anywhere and start talking and people are going to give you their opinion on the Iditarod, on the mushers, you name it.

My Yellow Bowl, limited edition print, 1995.

CHAPTER 19

Stan
HOOLEY

xecutive director of the Iditarod Trail Sled Dog Race since 1993, Stan Hooley came to Alaska from Indiana and is the longest serving executive in the history of the race. Hooley has presided over a period of extended growth for the event—his marching orders from the start—and is the face of the event to the public.

Business acumen and administration skills are what Hooley is chiefly tasked with bringing to the race rather than on-the-trail expertise. He is the marketing leader under whose watch the race has expanded and become better known throughout the United States and internationally.

Growing up in Elkhart in northern Indiana, Hooley then attended Manchester College. A one-time college football player as an offensive guard at the NCAA Division III level, Hooley specialized in athletic administration professionally. Before joining the Iditarod staff in Wasilla he worked for the Amateur Athletic Union of the United States as executive director and was brought to Alaska to infuse new blood and new thinking into the Iditarod. For most of its early existence the Iditarod had been a mom-and-pop operation with few full-time employees and a rough-edged storefront office, presided over by a board of directors featuring several mushers.

While still under the sway of a board and with mushers still having a say-so in operations the Iditarod has grown into a much bigger business with national and international advertisers and larger purses for mushers over the last twenty years.

I had been fascinated with Alaska all of my life, since I was a child. I was in Indiana, but my first real knowledge of the Iditarod dates to 1985 and came about in a fashion as it did for millions of other people. That's when Libby Riddles won the race and became the first woman champion.

Then there was this extreme curiosity as to what this event was all about. It just piqued my interest. I was the youngest person to hold the job as executive director of the Amateur Athletic Union and I was living in Indianapolis. At that time I was running around the country—way too much—working with different sporting events and I was transitioning to working on various marketing partnerships.

I traveled to New York City quite often, usually a week a month, to work with an agency and it just so happened that group had a connection to the Iditarod. So every month I'd walk into their office, and like any good marketing agency they had their clients' stuff all over the walls. There was the AAU stuff and there were Iditarod images. When I was waiting for a meeting to start I was always looking at this wall.

Marketing partnerships help make special events work and I was working with track and field or basketball or gymnastics, obviously sports that are a lot different than the Iditarod. But they all have one common thread and that's extreme competitiveness. I would be in this office and over the course of a few years I would make a lot of comments about my fascination with Alaska and the Iditarod.

In the fall of 1992 and into the spring of 1993, the Iditarod Trail Committee appointed a committee to search for a new executive director and it had the theme of, "We're going to break the mold. We're going to look outside of ourselves a little bit and see who might be interested in this job." The search got underway and one day I'm sitting in my office in Indianapolis and the phone rings. It was the Alaska search committee. Somehow my name had ended up on a list. It was pretty much, "We don't know if this guy is interested, but here's somebody you ought to at least talk to." That's how the conversation started. Another few months passed and I had traveled to interview with the board.

So I came here and the thought of living in Alaska and pursuing my passion of chasing oversized and overweight rainbow trout just seemed a little too much to resist. Of course I was fascinated with the prospect of seeing what I could do for the race.

At the time I didn't know how many people had gone through this chair in a short period of time and how unstable the organization was. I think I was the fourth or fifth person in a span of just a few years, so the job came with some risk. I left something behind that was enjoyable except at that time I had become a bit weary of the travel demands.

With the AAU I hired on at what I call the bottom of the food chain in 1985 and for the first few years was working with cities and local community organizations planning different championship events. I was a sports coordinator, an administrative type, and then I was executive director. That's what required a lot of traveling. My whole career there was 1985 to 1992. To this day I don't really care for airports and rental cars and freeways and hotel rooms. I started in 1993 and twenty years have gone by. It's like a lot of things when you slow down long enough to reflect, you go, "Where did the twenty years go?"

I came as a thirty-five-year-old. I've got one new knee and I'm getting another new one soon. I've played hard and am paying the price for it at this stage of my life, but I wouldn't have it any other way. It's been an enjoyable experience.

The romance of the Iditarod lured me in. It grips you as a casual fan. And it still grips you as a more knowledgeable race fan. It's an event like no other. I've worked for some pretty big events. I have some pretty big events in my background. But there's an element unique to this.

I played football in college, pretty much back in the leather helmet era, it seems. I have to think of it that way since people go, "Oh, you played football?" It was a long time ago, but it was enjoyable. That's one of the reasons I have the knees I have now. Then I started in with coaching. My alma mater hired me. I started out with some guys who are still in the business and some who have done great things in coaching. Some of them look at me and go, "Geez, I wish I had gotten out of coaching and done what you've done over the years." And I say to them, "I'd give anything to have a whistle around my neck and a clipboard stuck in the back of my shorts and be able to go out and scream at people all day."

For them, it's more because they wish they had a more stable life and didn't always have to be putting the FOR SALE sign up in their front yard. You're there as long as you're successful and once the win-loss record goes, so does your residence.

Several things make the Iditarod an event like no other, as I said. It's a combination of a lot of things, including The Last Frontier, the weather, the challenge against the elements, man and dog together. I believe the focal point is the four-legged athletes. It's hard to wrap your head around what these dogs are capable of doing given the proper nutrition and training. I refer to successful mushers as being people that are expert in a lot of different areas, whether it's nutrition or psychology. The successful ones are very well-versed in the medical aspects of caring for these dogs and getting them to perform at their optimum level. The dogs are what people relate to the most. They relate to the mushers and their success, too. The lifestyles mushers lead are what many folks in busy, urban areas revere for a lot of reasons. It's almost a jealousy. It's like, "I wish I had the guts to live that life."

There is a sense of freedom, of liberation attached to that lifestyle. That's what they think, but they don't realize that it's a very structured environment. I grew up on a dairy farm so my early years were very structured taking care of animals. These dogs are the same way. You are married to that kennel.

The average person doesn't know that. They don't know what it takes to maintain a kennel for 365 days a year, whether it's a racing kennel or a recreational kennel. So there's a bit of a disconnect there. Nonetheless, it's part of the reason why people admire the race as they do. Then you throw in the backdrop of Alaska, the venue where it is contested, and with those ingredients there's nothing like it.

Plus, there's competition. People like to see who goes the fastest. We talk a lot about the volunteers who make this race happen—and bear in mind we can never talk about those volunteers too much. You hear varying numbers, but I'm going to say the number of volunteers for the Iditarod each year is between 1,400 and 1,500. Probably 600 or 700 of them are Anchorage based. The opportunities to go out along the trail are in smaller numbers. They've become an extended family of sorts. They'll carve out a week or two of their existence each year to be part of this race. Other events I've been associated with people do that once or twice and scratch it off their bucket list. Not here.

We have people come back and do what they do for this race year after year after year. There's a bonding element in this race that I don't think exists at any other event. Part of the reason is the volunteers, the race staff, race officials, and mushers are all working together to get to Nome. It's not just race officials—they're busy being tasked with enforcing the rules of the rulebook—but the volunteers play a big role in getting these teams to Nome. There's much more of a participatory blend with everybody who's involved in this. I think that's what creates the bond between people.

That is a lot of volunteers. Some of the obvious jobs are the checkpoint personnel relaying race data back to communications. The checkers themselves are checking dog teams in and out. There are dropped dog handlers. There are veterinarians. There are pilots. There are trailbreakers. Then in Anchorage you've got volunteers working twenty-four hours a day entering race data to regurgitate race updates that update the million and a half people who are focused specifically on our website for two weeks straight. I've got people answering the telephone. The Anchorage start itself is a huge effort. The number of people working in some traffic control or security capacity is significant. The number of staging coordinators working with the start coordinator to get the teams to the starting line is large. That's where these numbers come from. I'm going to say off the top of my head that Anchorage alone probably accounts for a third or so of the volunteers.

I fantasize about being out on the trail during the race more than I actually get out there. This race moves so fast. From the standpoint of all the things we're engaged in to make this race run smoothly, I have found it better in terms of managing things not to spend as much time as I otherwise would love to on the trail during the race. I do take one overnight trip on the trail with a group of our race sponsors, but it's a quick overnight and back. For the last couple of years it's been to McGrath and back. We've been there for the presentation of the Pen Air Spirit of Alaska Award and enjoyed the auction at McGuire's Tavern. We soak up a little of the local fun that happens there and get to know the people a little better. But it's better for the race if there is no time during the race when people are trying to call me that they can't reach me.

The ball needs to continue rolling and whether it's being available via cell phone or landline or SAT phone or Internet—all of those things at one point or another play a significant role. I need to stay in touch. This thing moves so fast—that's one of the things that has changed from a racing standpoint since I got involved—is how the speed has changed.

I've been around for twenty years, but the big-picture feeling of excitement I get relates to the dogs themselves. In Anchorage you would expect these dogs to be amped up, fully charged, excitable, ready to go. You would expect them to be lunging in their harnesses, jumping three feet in the air, barking, yipping, wasting a lot of energy, which they do. What you don't necessarily expect is that when you're 1,049 miles away from Anchorage, standing on Front Street in Nome under the burled arch, and a dog team and musher finish, as they're going through checking gear, going through the interview process, snacking their dogs, to see dogs banging away in their harnesses, yelling, yelping, trying to pull the snow hook, saying it's time to go. I'm getting goose bumps thinking about it. I don't know if they're ready to go another thousand miles, but they're ready to go further.

A lot of studies have been completed on these dogs now and one thing that our antagonists, or somebody who has questions about what sled dogs are capable of, need to see is the start of the race and they need to see the finish of the race and put those two things together and then wrap their minds around the thought that the last nine or ten days those dogs traveled one thousand miles, yet here they are ready to go further.

Some people don't want to see it and my response to some of the doubters is that everybody is entitled to their opinion, but I don't consider it a valid opinion until you make a valid effort to understand the event. That little fuzzy critter that's lying at your feet in an apartment in name a city, it's a mistake to compare that dog with a sled dog when you're trying to understand what the Iditarod is about.

Sometimes unusual things happen during the race. There are a lot of colorful people involved in this organization that love to have fun in a good way. Sometimes the weather determines things. I was so excited to be on the trail in 1994 for my first race.

I recall something my first year. No matter how much time you spend in the woods and exploring, when you fly into a remote checkpoint like Cripple and it's fifty below, and there is no real heat source, it's cold. There was no real shelter other than a log cabin with some straw on the ground and I was going to spend forty-eight hours there. Until you've done that you never really truly understand what the mushers and their teams go through for two weeks at a time.

Our good friends at GCI had just become a sponsor and it was the first year they were going to present the GCI Dorothy Page Halfway Award. It was my first year to see the trail and I had every bit of cold-weather gear that I owned with me. The temperature got down to minus fifty and there was a volunteer—I wish I could remember his name—that had a bottle of Jack Daniels. It was a situation where you had to get up and just move around every so often because it was so cold. There was no heat and we slept on straw on the ground on top of snow. It was a fitful night's sleep and in the morning the bottle of Jack Daniels was frozen solid. I thought, *How cold does it have to be for that to happen?*

We had a fire going the night before and that morning I got up and was restarting that fire. Everything had burned down and there were just a couple of coals to work with. I was stirring them with a stick and I saw something else in there with the ashes that was kind of heavy. The guy at the check-point had brought a pistol and the gun was in the fire. It was a Ruger Red Hawk and the wooden handle was burned off. I backed up since I thought it was going to start going off. Turns out it wasn't loaded. Apparently while he was tending the fire it fell out of the pocket of his coat.

Already, on my first trip on the trail, I was starting to feel like a character in a Jack London story.

CHAPTER 20

Sebastian
SCHNUELLE

I t's difficult to keep up with Sebastian Schnuelle. He was born in Germany, lived in Whitehorse, Yukon Territory, works summers in the Juneau, Alaska, area, and now has a cabin in the Fairbanks area. The common theme, once he came to the North Country from Europe, is dogs.

Schnuelle, whose trademark wild hair sticking out in all directors, much like Harpo Marx, identifies him from a distance, still maintains a team that he uses for backcountry trips, but has sworn off competing in the Yukon Quest and the Iditarod for now. However, he remains close to the sport and during a typical Iditarod he travels the trail by snowmachine as a photographer and writer.

Born in Wuppertal, Germany, forty-four years ago, Schnuelle studied to be an environmental engineer before moving to Canada in search of adventure in 1997. He alighted in Ontario and made his way west, settling in the Yukon for years, where he took up mushing, started a kennel, and competed in middle-distance races before joining the one-thousand-mile club in the Yukon Quest and then the Iditarod.

Beginning in 2005, Schnuelle, who is regarded as one of the friendliest of mushers, competed in the Iditarod seven times. In 2009 he finished second and he owns three top-ten finishes. That same year Schnuelle won the Quest title. Schnuelle won the Iditarod's Humanitarian Award in 2010.

I still have my cabin in Whitehorse, but I bought a property in Fairbanks from people I knew. It came with all of the furniture, all of the dog equipment, dog sleds, there was food in the cupboard. They even left my Diet Coke for me when I moved in. I just took my dogs with me and my one trailer and truck from Whitehorse.

Growing up in Germany I liked dogs, but I never did anything with dogs and I never thought about having any. I didn't even have a pet. I was working as an environmental engineer and I was sent to Toronto to work on a project and when it was time to leave a coworker said, "Sebastian, you can't leave here without saying you've never been on a dog team." So he took me out for a dog-team ride. I go out on a Sunday afternoon and I thought, *This is pretty cool.* I loved it. I was twenty-four at the time.

So that winter I got back to Germany and I had eight weeks of vacation coming and they said, "You've got to take it now or we're going to kill it." I didn't know what I was going to do with all that time in the winter. I wasn't a winter sports person. Remembering the dog-sled ride, I booked a weeklong dog trip in Canada in a national park and totally fell in love with it.

That was just a week and I still had all of this vacation after I went back to Germany again. I called the dog-mushing company back and asked if they had any longer trips. They had a three-week expedition going to Hudson Bay and I said, "Sign me up, I'm going." It was even better. It was further out there. I ended up quitting my job in Germany and applying for permanent residency in Canada.

I started working for Chocpaw Expeditions doing adventure trips in Algonquin Provincial Park in Ontario. I believe the company was named because of a brown Siberian being its first dog. They're still in business, a very big business, with 350 dogs. I worked for them one winter and I've always been a water person and in summer I led paddling trips on the McKenzie River. After doing that I hitchhiked all over and that's how I saw the Yukon. As soon as I saw that place I said, "I'm not going back to Ontario. No way." And I went to Whitehorse in 1997.

At that point I knew nothing about the Yukon Quest and the Iditarod. Nothing. Once you're there you're going to hear about it. Very foolishly I signed up for the Quest in 1999. In hindsight I'm amazed they let me get to the starting line. Joe May, who is a great guy, was the race marshal and by the time I got to Circle he wasn't leaving me very many options. He goes, "Sebastian, I think you can scratch, and if you don't, I'll withdraw you."

Of course at the time I was disappointed, pissed off. I didn't have any money, so I was hugely in debt. It was *Now what?* And you never have a second chance to make a first impression. This wasn't very good. It took me five years to recuperate from that scratch, mainly moneywise. But I also realized I needed to run many more mid-distance races for experience, which I should have done before. I signed up again in 2004 and at the time my motto was "Unfinished business." I really just wanted to finish that one Quest.

That year I finished tenth and immediately after I finished I thought, *Never again.* But by June or July I was thinking, *Ah, maybe one more time.* I also had a German friend who said, "Sebastian, why don't you sign up for the Iditarod, too?" That's why, in 2005, with just one Quest finish I was foolish enough to sign up for both. Once again I had no clue what I got myself into. At that time I had a pretty big tour business in Whitehorse and it completely screwed up everything when I did both. I had a relationship and that went to hell and in essence doing both races almost caused me to sell the business because she wanted half.

I had to decide which direction to go in and I ended up entering seven Quests and finishing six and I did pretty much the same thing with the Iditarod entering every year. By 2010 I was thinking I'd had enough of this racing. I'd always been a camper. I did well, winning the Quest and finishing second in the Iditarod, but although I am very competitive I like Bush camping. Racing really became more like a job. I had to train, train, train and I just didn't like it. I don't regret racing, but it got to the point where if I wanted to stay near the top I had to continue like that.

In 2009 I finished second in the Iditarod and I was coming off a win in the Quest. That was a totally unusual win in the Quest. Pretty much all of the way on the trail I thought I was going to finish fourth or fifth. The other guys were too far ahead of me and my goal in the Quest that year was not to win, but just to be better in the Iditarod. I had been tenth and there was a lot more money in the Iditarod. I just wanted to run strong in the Quest. By the time I got to Circle the three mushers ahead of me had already left and I thought, *That's fine with me.* The lead was at least eight hours.

I was just totally enjoying myself. I never even thought about racing. I came into Central and it was the same scenario. There were no other teams there. I was going to leave at three o'clock in the morning, but when my wakeup call came at two o'clock. I thought, *Aw, give me another two hours sleep.* Brent Sass was coming behind me, but I thought he wasn't going to be able to catch me. It all worked in my favor. Those other guys ahead of me all had problems with their dog teams or the weather. William Kleedehn had trouble with his dogs. Hugh Neff and Jon Little were just inching along. You could see where they had bedded down. You could see where they had been trying to walk up the hill on Eagle Summit. Then my basic instincts kicked in and I saw racing opportunity.

Once again Eagle Summit changed things. Up until then my racing strategy had been, "I don't care where everybody else is." You need fuel in the tank going over that summit. Sometimes, even if you have fuel in the tank you're not going to make it up there. The thing is pretty steep. Going north, if you have a tired team, you don't get away with it. On Eagle Summit, if the dogs are too tired physically it stops you. They can't do it even if they mentally want to. And Hugh had a penalty.

Overall, it was surprising that I was in first and it was pretty cool. Hugh really had the fastest team, but he got a penalty for running on the road. I think it should have been a monetary penalty, not a two-hour time penalty. But it is what it is.

It's definitely cool that I won the Yukon Quest. It was not that it was a dream of a lifetime like it is for people who have had it as a goal for so long, but it is definitely pretty cool. I also had a second team, a young team in the Quest, for the experience. I had strong dogs and I went right into the Iditarod. I realized running both races back to back was better for the strength of the dogs.

At the time, I'd say Lance Mackey, Hugh, Hans Gatt, Ken Anderson, and I were the ones who had kind of clued into the fact that back-to-back running was good for the dogs. My plan was to pick the best dogs from the Quest teams, figuring I should have about twenty finishers, and then pick my Iditarod team from that. Normally, you have to ease your way into the start of the Iditarod. They have to make that metabolic switch or they become alligators and eat everything. But I thought they could put the pedal to the metal right away. The day after the Quest ended I took my team out and ran them about another fifty miles. Most people would have thought they needed to rest all week. We kept them at a high metabolic rate. They were happy to go. It was just another run to them, just another run of the sort they had been doing. For the dogs it was easy.

There were a lot of discussions with my handlers and others and they tried to talk me out of it. I said, "No, this is how I want to have those dogs come into the race." I had twenty-one finishers in the Quest. It used to be that if you pulled into Skwentna on the first run in the Iditarod pretty fast you paid for that at the end of the race. Not only did I push it to Skwentna in one run, I pulled out of there after two hours and twenty minutes. I remember Ken Anderson had just parked next to me and I started bootie-ing up and he said something like, "What on earth are you doing?" I was so convinced about what the dogs could do that I was going for it. My plan was only to finish in the top five in the Iditarod. I didn't really think about winning it that year.

My mind-set never did change on that point. In hindsight, it could have, but unfortunately not. I don't want to say that's why I ended up second, but I ended up second by seven hours. The deciding moment came much later in the race. But that Iditarod was one of those magic carpet rides. There were no injuries because those dogs were absolutely bulletproof. I had sixteen dogs for a long time and I ended up being on the Bering Sea Coast with fifteen. In 2008 I made a mistake from lack of experience and I stayed in Shaktoolik. So this time, with the team I had, I had a plan that I wasn't stopping no matter what. I pulled into Shaktoolik and I declared I was going through, but what hadn't registered in my mind, in my ignorance, was that there was a pretty good storm raging out there.

One year I screwed up because I stopped there, so this year I'm going. I got out there and it was blowing and I thought, *Ooh. What the hell did you get yourself into?* That's when I realized why Jeff King and Mitch Seavey were staying back. I didn't want to pull over and stop. What happened was it was blowing so hard the dogs' eyelids were crusting shut. They were running and all of a sudden we would be off the trail. So I did stop and decrust them. It was getting more and more difficult. I was trying to get to Koyuk and I was thinking that this could really turn sour.

When I got to Shaktoolik Lance Mackey was the only team ahead of me and he had gone through. There were about eleven teams within a half hour of one another. It was incredibly close, but the payoff for the places was like a difference of $30,000 so I thought, *Shut up and be willing to suffer.*

I didn't know who was coming behind me, but I thought John Baker would. It was a tough run over to Koyuk and I had it because of one dog, Finn. Finn was in the lead and all of the other dogs kept shutting down on me, but when they didn't want to go Finn would forcefully jerk and get going. That ended up being a long run.

From Unalakleet it normally takes like six hours to Koyuk. I think it took me nine and a half and I already had a long run into Shaktoolik before. It was a monster long run. When I got to Koyuk Lance was already there. The only other thing moving behind me was John Baker. Nobody else wanted to start out. I'm in second place and that was pretty cool. But that's when my racing instinct wasn't there enough. I thought I could win it because Lance was still there. Actually, Lance came out and talked to me. With the experience he had he probably knew I wasn't trying hard to catch him. Lance stayed another three and a half hours, I think, but I ended up staying there for twelve hours.

It's like forever. I got into Koyuk about five o'clock in the afternoon and I ended up leaving the next morning with John Baker. We had agreed on running together. That showed my confidence. Lance left three and a half hours after I got in. That would have been my chance if I went with him. At least I should have only let him go ahead of me for an hour or so. That's why I say mentally it wasn't in my thoughts that I could win the Iditarod. I wasn't mentally there. Once you have a lot of sleep it was like, *What on earth was I thinking?*

I had fifteen dogs, so even if not every dog was completely up to it I could have dropped the ones that couldn't go and had twelve. That was more than most other people had. It was fatigue and it was also lack of experience after just two races. At the time I was tired. When we left Koyuk I think John had nine dogs and I had fourteen. We arranged to run together, but I thought whenever I wanted to I could pull away from him because I had so many more dogs. The other guys were like twelve hours behind us, so my thinking was that second place was secure. I didn't want to screw it up. It came with $60,000 and I didn't want to blow it because I really, really needed that money. I was tired and I was content with the money. I wasn't chasing Lance. Of course, now in hindsight I think, *You idiot!*

When I started racing and did the Quest and Iditarod and my relationship went to hell, I basically said I was going into racing for six years and that was going to be it. I looked at it as one life cycle of a dog team. I've never been a big fan of breeding. I knew I had a decent team and the dogs were young. My thinking was that when they were old enough to retire I would stop. I won the Quest and I could say that I got what I wanted. I won one of them. I had never had a dead dog. I had a pretty clean career. After finishing second, though, I felt I was right in the hunt.

But my life wasn't going well and I should have taken that as a sign. My 2010 season was all screwed up. I finished seventh in the Iditarod and I was disgusted with myself. Before that I would have been happy with seventh, but at that point I was saying, *Why did you screw up this bad?* It was really a very good finish since some of the dogs were too old. Stubborn as I was, I said I was going to do another one in 2011 and once again had horrible preparation.

I think I went through fourteen dog handlers that season. No, I didn't shoot them one at a time. I wish. I finished second in the Quest and everybody saw how great I did, but I was completely unhappy the whole season. I kept asking myself, *What on earth are you doing out there? Why are you doing this again?* So I knew it was over. It had gone away from enjoyment to pure ego. But I had trained and spent the money and was entered. So I just went. My dogs were ancient. Some of them were nine years old. Before the Iditarod, the musher Gerry Willomitzer made a joke. He said, "Sebastian, you should get a wheelchair for your dogs."

They just weren't fast enough anymore. If you had patience they ran perfectly fine. They were happy. They would eat. They were actually fat. They had so much experience, but the actual traveling speed was slow as molasses. We went out and had a good run, but everybody just outran me. I was only resting three and a half hours. We finished sixth. After the 2011 Iditarod I knew I was done racing.

It's permanent in terms of racing, but not permanent in the sense that I absolutely love the trip. I really enjoy the community, the Iditarod family, the snowmachiners, the people, the scenery, all of it. At some point I'm going to show up with a team and just do it. I may finish in fortieth place, I don't care. I'll just do it for the trip.

Maybe I can do the race as a reporter-photographer on the back of a dog team instead of on the back of a snowmachine. I would be an official starter, but I could set up at a checkpoint and blog and upload things on Facebook. Right now under the rules in the Quest you can't do that. If they gave me permission as an official competitor and somehow I finished in the money I would put the money back in the pot.

I want to stay involved, but I don't want to race like I was because when I did I had no other life. I went through two relationships doing that. It's like that with anything, no matter if you are a human athlete running marathons, if you do something to the extreme all other aspects of life suffer because you put all of your time into it.

My parents are getting old. I'm flying over to Germany to visit for a month. I couldn't do that before because of the training. I'm over the hump as far as being competitive, but I might just show up to run the race without racing hard-core. There's got to be another motivation besides ego. If I won the Quest again I would win $19,000, so I would lose money. I've been there and done it. Just being a two-time winner of the Quest is not enough motivation.

I had two clients rent teams to do the Yukon Quest 300. Maybe I'll do that to be out on the trail with them. But I love it now that when I get up in the morning I can go, *Hmm, do I feel like training or not?* It's not like when you have a schedule where you've got to do it. It didn't bother me when I was into it hard-core. If you're truly believing in something the energy increases. Now looking back, I'm like, *Wow, I did all that?* Now if it's forty below I'm thinking, *Oh, God.* Before it wasn't even a thought. When you have a goal and you truly love it and believe in it, the negative parts are gone. There are none. I have to admit that something I miss in my life is the intensity, the next goal.

It was enjoyable being surrounded by intense, driven people, a different part of society, not the people lazing around on the couch or drifting along in life. Mushers are interesting people. They are driven and focused. It's almost the same for some volunteers and people who have been race judges or trailbreakers for decades.

Something I took from competing in the Quest and the Iditarod is that you can pretty much do anything if you set your mind to it as long as you truly believe in it. If you don't, you'd better stay away from it because it's very, very difficult. The intensity is pretty neat. It's pretty neat when you're in it, but when you're over it, it's like, *Whoa, what the heck was I thinking?*

Some people are in the Iditarod forever, but I have to say I'm lucky because I have another passion. I love sailing and being in Southeast Alaska in the summer I do a lot of that. You've got to have a second passion. Now I can say that slowly photography is becoming a passion. I am drifting into that. It's taking over. That's why I don't have to fulfill a need with racing the Iditarod.

I have to redefine myself. If I'm not the racing Sebastian, who the hell am I? Which direction should I go? I'm at a stage in life where I'm doing tourism and I'm doing the photography. I'm very happy.

You only make money if you stay on top and I had to continue training hard to make money. In 2011 I finished second in the Quest and sixth in the Iditarod and I lost $40,000 that year. Effectively, I had $40,000 less in my account in March than I had in September. That shows how expensive it is to race.

The costs came from training, feeding, vehicle breakdown, everything. I thought, *I just can't continue to go that route. Enough of the racing.* But it was sort of a lie that I could completely step away. The writing and picture taking came up for *Iditarod Insider* and I did the race on a snowmachine.

Now I plan to just go out in the woods with the dogs and in the summer work on the Hubbard Glacier near Juneau with tourists. Since 2007 I was sending my dogs there and didn't go myself. Then by 2010 I started working on the glacier. Basically, I worked six days on the glacier, one off, but I've gotten stuck more and more in administration and now I'm six days off the glacier and one on.

Two Tenors, painting, 2008.

CHAPTER 21

Hugh NEFF

rowing up in the Chicago area after being born in Chatta-
nooga, Tennessee, Hugh Neff, forty-seven, became enamored
of the north by reading Jack London fiction and true-life stories of modern mushers. A golf caddy when he was in high school where he
crossed paths with comedic actor Bill Murray, Neff attended the University
of Illinois. He later made his way to Alaska and became a dog handler to
learn the tricks of the trade.

Desperate to hurry the process along he entered his first one-thousand-
mile races on a shoestring budget and using others' loaner dogs. But he got
better and better at mushing, picking up experience by racing the Yukon
Quest and the Iditarod Trail Sled Dog Race year after year. The 2014 Iditarod was Neff's tenth venture on the trail and after that mushing season he
also had fourteen Quests under his belt since 2000.

Neff has lived in Alaska since 1995, in Anchorage, Skagway, and Tok, his
current home, and built his kennel from scratch into one that can contend
for championships in both one-thousand-mile races. In 2011 he finished fifth
in the Iditarod. He was also the race's 2004 rookie of the year. Neff won the
2012 Quest title.

In recent years Neff has toured several states to give Iditarod presentations and tell stories about his Laughing Eyes Kennel, including visits to his

own old elementary school in Illinois. He stresses the value of reading to schoolchildren and often is seen wearing a Doctor Seuss Cat in the Hat hat. He has also written a book about his mushing adventures titled *Tails of the Gypsy Musher, Alaska and Beyond.*

Even before I came to Alaska, all my friends in Chicago were calling me "Mr. Alaska" because all I could talk about was Alaska.

In sports I grew up watching Michael Jordan and the Bulls win NBA championships, but when I finished college I didn't know what I wanted to do. After a while my dad said that I needed to figure out what I wanted to do in this world. What I did sort of shocked him. I think he kind of wanted me to go into politics or something and he wondered what my college education went for.

I had dogs my whole life growing up in Illinois. When I was a little kid in the sandbox in the backyard I got bitten by a dog named Scotty. Later, I told all my friends that's when I became part dog.

When I first came to Alaska I got a job in Anchorage working on a slime line for a seafoods company by the airport. I was living out of a campground with no money to my name and went downtown and saw an Iditarod Show at the Fourth Avenue Theatre. I remember seeing Martin Buser in it and he seemed totally out of it at a checkpoint, suffering, but he looked like he was having fun at what he was doing. It seemed that whole adventure was what it was about for me.

When I moved to Alaska I didn't know anybody and I got lucky and met one of the most famous sprint-mushing families. They taught me how to mush. I did things backwards. Instead of learning about long-distance mushing, I learned about sprint mushing first. I was in Tanana and I got a job working for Curtis Erhart, and Gareth Wright was nearby. That's where my true Alaska education began when I left the road system and got out in the Bush. That background may not have been great for learning how to do long-distance races, but it taught me how to travel, be on my own, and be self-sufficient. There was a lot of hardship in the beginning, but that's how you learn.

You have to be alone a lot when you are a musher, alone with the dogs.

Wherever I go in Alaska and to make speeches, I'm a pretty well-known person and I can talk in front of thousands of people, but usually in my day-to-day living I hide from people. I go through life and I do my things in my own little world. I spend a lot of time with the dogs and the more you get into it the easier it is to relate to the dogs. If you want to be a great dog musher you've got to totally focus on them.

Doing a lot of one-thousand-mile races, that's always been my deal. Winning the Iditarod would be nice, but everybody has their time. Every year I want to be the guy out there on the sled. It's a greedy thing, but it's a good thing to be greedy about. I skipped the Iditarod in 2013 because I traveled. I went to Norway and raced over there. I was the first Alaskan since Joe Redington to be over there racing. They treated me great.

Nobody in the Iditarod could figure out why I did it. They didn't realize to me it's not just all racing. Right before Joe Redington passed away, in his eighties, he signed up to do the Quest. He was an explorer at heart. I think those mushers who don't try it are doing mushing a disservice by not doing a Quest.

In 2000 when I was a rookie I was a complete novice. I was borrowing dogs from people a couple of weeks before the race. I started the Quest with only ten dogs out of Fairbanks. The limit was fourteen. Three dogs that I borrowed only made it about three hundred miles, so for the last seven hundred miles I only had seven dogs and I came in thirteenth out of thirty teams. That's when it taught me it isn't about numbers, it's about having a team.

I learned a lot. I was with Frank Turner, the great Quest musher and I said, "Mr. Turner, how do I stop hallucinating?" He says, "Have you tried drinking any water yet?" I really hadn't. I was dehydrated big-time. You learn through the school of hard knocks. Another reason why I race so much is so I can keep learning. I've done quite a few one-thousand-mile races, but I don't think I'm anywhere close to my potential yet. It was a beautiful thing I remember Susan Butcher doing. Right at the finish line one year she started making a list of what she could do better the next time.

When I'm racing I'm racing against people. I pretend I'm racing against those people that were my heroes from reading books. The Butchers, the Osmars, the Swensons. Sonny Lindner is a big hero of mine. Not necessarily all people who win. People like Herbie Nayokpuk. Those are the people I want to emulate because they're the true essence of the Iditarod.

It's just their spirit and how they represent Alaska. To them it's just about being good dog men and not about what place they came in. It's good to be competitive, but dog mushing isn't racing, it's a religion. When a lot of us are together we're not talking about what place we came in, but we're talking about each other's dogs, like, "You should have seen my dog do this." We put the dogs on a pedestal.

After the 2000 Quest I knew it would be a long time before I won any races. You have to go through the phase that all young mushers do and learn, learn, from other people. When I'm around mushers I'm always talking to the older guys. They're the guys to get advice from, mostly about what not to do. I was lucky I got to work for some of the top Native mushers like Jerry Riley and Gareth Wright. They sat me down and told me stories about what the weather was like and things like that.

My rookie year in the Iditarod, going down the Yukon River I was in the top twenty. I took a break in the middle of the day because it was hot. I was just short of Nulato and there was a guy on the side of the river with his son with a snowmachine just watching the teams go by. I stopped and said, "Hey, do you mind if I snack my dogs?" We were chitchatting for a while and when I was getting ready to go I said, "What's your name?" He said, "Hugh." Then I looked at the kid and said, "What's his name?" And he goes, "Hugh Jr." Dude, we had three Hughs in the middle of nowhere. That was the weirdest experience.

The coolest thing that ever happened in another race was through the Internet. I was in White Mountain starting my eight-hour layover and as I pulled in a guy said, "Hey, a friend of yours wanted me to give this to you." It was three o'clock in the morning and it was a canister with coffee and I had been dying of thirst.

I think all mushers have something they bring to the table, especially those guys that are the true wilderness warriors of the past. They didn't have trails like we do now. The race is faster, but it's more easily managed than it used to be. I'm never going to be a guy who is all about winning. I just want to keep racing and having fun. I'm in my mid-forties now, but that's the beauty of watching these older guys like Jeff King who are ten years older. They're definitely good role models. My whole goal is not necessarily to come in first or second in the Quest, but to be in the top three, the top five, for my whole career. If I could do that I wouldn't even care if I won another race.

For me, it's more of a deal where I want to reach my potential. That's why I want to win the Iditarod. Not to win, but to have that magic carpet ride that Martin said. I've been close. I've had some nice runs on the Bering Sea Coast and the Coast is what separates the Iditarod from the Quest. I was almost going to move there a couple of years ago just to train and get more comfortable with that area. I don't really have the nervousness I used to leaving Shaktoolik and Koyuk. The first couple of years in the Iditarod I was nervous going out there by myself. In 2012 I blew right through that area and everybody else stayed there for like fifteen hours. I was out there in a storm myself and it felt great actually.

Sometimes being out on the trail in the Quest or Iditarod it's almost a religious experience for me. It's very emotional with the dogs. Sometimes I've cried and sometimes I just have this euphoria. But in 2011 in the Quest I had a horrible experience on Eagle Summit. I had a huge lead and then I had a dog perish. It regurgitated. It was the worst experience of my life since my mom died. So the rest of the race I could feel that dog's spirit with us. It was almost like I had an extra dog bringing us to the finish line.

There was a lot of trauma. When I crossed the finish line I raised my hands in the air and screamed, "Geronimo!" I don't like to be a Bible thumper and talk religion, but I definitely think that you feel another presence when you're out in the wilderness. There is a special essence there. Sometimes it makes you feel like a flea on a dog. You feel a part of that wilderness. That's why I keep coming back. I would feel bad if I didn't race.

I love the Quest. It's more of a low-key, local race where they want to be organized, but just never really are. It never really evolves, but it's always there. I love the trail. I love Dawson City. The Iditarod is more corporate oriented. There's more money in it. I'd rather be the underdog. I'm still as poor as I was when I moved here. I keep on throwing all the money back into the dream.

My best Iditarod was 2011 when I came in fifth. I came in twenty-second as a rookie in 2004. I had an outfit just like one of my heroes, Dick Mackey, with a green Iditarod patch on the side. He was my idol. Dick and the whole family [Rick, Lance] had so much energy to take on the hardness of the race. Doug Swingley said long-distance mushing is all about time management. You've got to learn how to be patient and not so hyper all the time, which I tend to get in races. Sometimes you need to hang back a little bit.

I was rookie of the year, but I think I could have done better. I had a lot better mushers flying by me on the Coast because my dogs weren't used to it. That whole year I just focused on Timmy Osmar, who taught me a lot on the Quest. He's just an amazing guy with an amazing dog mind. So I just followed him around and he left me in the dust once we got to the Coast.

A lot of being new to mushing is knowing how to run the dog team. You do that by slowing down. Most younger mushers think you go fast in the beginning. That's just going to throw your dogs off. There's a different type of intensity in the Iditarod than there is in the Quest. In the Iditarod you want to hide from the big names because you get stuck in their soap opera world and they're just going to use you on the trail. You run your own race. That's how you succeed. That's what I'm trying to do, have my own strategy. I'm also sort of anti-techno while everyone has all these new gadgets. I don't even have a cell phone. I don't want to be out there listening to music on headphones and using a GPS. I want to be like the old-school mushers. I don't need to be jamming to AC/DC or whatever. I think it takes away from being out in the woods. What are you doing this for?

Really my love of Alaska is my big thing. I love to be out in the beautiful mountains. I may even love the Yukon better than Alaska. I kind of want to move back into the Bush off the road system, but it's sort of hard to do being a racer. I moved to Tok because there aren't any other mushers there. I want to do this for a long time and I like guys like Joe Redington, who was mushing in his eighties, and Jim Lanier. Those are guys that I want to be like. They're amazing. It's learning to control your body as it ages because we're all still kids in our own minds.

I plan on winning the Iditarod. I hope I can. I have to say I will. That's what I'm thinking now. I have a very young dog yard right now. I switched my breeding lines over and went more to John Baker–type dogs. I have some of those and I bred them with Annie, my famous leader when I finished fifth. And I have some Hans Gatt dog lines. John Baker dogs have heavier coats. In Tok I live in a cold environment. It gets to be minus fifty. As you get older as a musher it's about attitude. It's the heart of the dogs and their being low maintenance. The profession gets more and more intense by the year. I don't have the greatest dog team. We all have the greatest dog team.

Some people just want to do the Iditarod once. It's part of their dream, their bucket list. It's doable. I just wish maybe the Iditarod came up with a different, smaller race for these other folks. I don't really put the Iditarod out there as a better race than all the others. I think every race should be a great race. I'm anti-Iditarod as the mecca of mushing. I think the mecca of mushing would be the All Alaska Sweepstakes of a hundred years ago. That's the original race.

There's a much bigger Native involvement in the Iditarod than there is in the Quest. They really like the Iditarod going through their villages and I dig the scene. I think that's what the Iditarod should really be about besides the dogs. I think that's why Joe Redington designed the whole thing. It's about celebrating Alaska and the lifestyle. We've got to interact as much as we can with the villagers. Unalakleet is another great place. All of the Natives are checking out your dogs and they're really into it. That's when you feel like you're really a part of something big.

I do love the Iditarod. We all love it for our own reasons. Mine is that I'm all about Alaska more than anything and as long as the Iditarod celebrates Alaska in the right fashion. It's not about musher infighting, or when it becomes too much about the musher and not about the dogs. We have these Hall of Fames and we should have dogs in those. We need to talk more about the dogs, I think. That's why people are attracted to the sport. It's the adventure, but it's the dogs that are getting us there.

I definitely see myself on the trail indefinitely. I'll never stop. Jeff King told me you've got to understand the big picture. You have to see your life and know what you want to get out of it and have a plan. When I beat Jeff King I know I'll have made it. I've been close a few times, and I've traveled with him a lot, but I've never beaten him in the Iditarod.

You've got to have your shtick if you're going to want to be in this long-term. That's why I created my Cat In The Hat character, the Gypsy Musher. As mushers we've got to be entertaining. We can't be so serious. We need the Joe Redingtons that are going to share our love of what we do. People want to know the inside scoop. They don't want us to be just a bunch of guys not talking to the media and just staring at our dogs the whole time. We're the go-betweens with the people watching and we've got to share our stories.

The funny thing is that I came to Alaska to live the simple life and it ain't that simple. I wanted to be a John Muir–type with a pack and a loaf of bread and be a hobo in the woods. But if you're going to have dogs. . . . I don't want to have to make money off my dogs. I'll make the money so I can do what I do with the dogs. I like to spend all summer with the dogs, not doing tourism rides. We're just hanging out in the yard. I'll take them on runs. I just think that's what being a true musher is about.

I'm on the road all of May. I do fifty to seventy talks a year. I get $500 to $600 an hour and sell books. Believe it or not, now I've got a poker tournament to raise money. A guy got in contact with me from Winter Park, Colorado, and said he wanted to have a poker tournament for me and a book signing.

One really interesting thing I run into is when I give talks in Europe—I just came back from Germany. As much as they want to know about dog mushing, they're fascinated by American Indians. If you go to anybody's house in Europe they have pictures and books everywhere about American Indians. I'm a Native wannabe and they want to hear all about life in the Alaska villages. I'm from Chicago and they don't want to know about Michael Jordan or Oprah, they all want to know about Al Capone and gangsters. Also about hunting. They love the adventure of the North. In Germany it seems like the Quest is bigger than the Iditarod. I'm not a real famous guy in Alaska. I can't get sponsors. I go to Europe and I'm a hero. My book is being printed in German. It's going to be in all of their outdoor stores, a chain like Cabela's. It's bizarre that I'm going to have much better sales in Germany than in America.

I came to Alaska without the Iditarod in mind. I came for a new life, away from big cities and traffic. I believe Alaska may not go over well with a lot of people. I don't think Alaska is like any other part of America. I think Alaska should be its own country.

CHAPTER 22

Newton MARSHALL

here is probably no more unlikely long-distance dog musher in the world than Newton Marshall since he hails from the beach paradise of Jamaica. Up until about five years ago Marshall, thirty, had never seen snow. Then through a combination of circumstances he ended up entering the 2009 Yukon Quest.

That figured to be a one-and-done deal for one-thousand-mile races and then back to the sands. Only Marshall developed a love for the sport and decided to try the Iditarod. In 2014 he was still out there in the wilderness plugging away in his fourth Iditarod.

Most of his countrymen don't know or understand what he is up to on his annual forays to the north, and perhaps the only winter sport comparison that can be made is the Jamaican bobsled team, which took the world by storm at the 1988 Winter Olympics in Calgary and returned to the Games in 2014 in Sochi, Russia.

Not surprisingly, when Marshall competed in the Quest as a rookie the first words he uttered at the first checkpoint on the trail when asked how it was going were, "It's cold." That was clearly an understatement for someone who grew up in a climate where it is usually in the eighties in the winter.

Marshall has made many friends in the North amongst race fans because of his open demeanor, infectious smile, and warm-weather country of origin.

I did not have a clue about anything that related to snow. I had never seen it, except on TV. Just seeing snow was a different experience for me. But what I really noticed was the cold. That is the big difference. This is not normal. I feel the cold.

When they were first putting together the Jamaican dog-sled team and trying me out, to get the idea of how dogs run, I went to Minnesota for the first time. This was just to see a dog-sled team, what it looked like and everything. That was the first time I encountered cold. It was like zero degrees at the end of March. I got off the plane with the camera guy and I felt this cold. I said to him, "Why do they have to turn up the air-conditioning so high?" He said, "That's not the AC, that's outside." Immediately my bladder just got weak. I had never felt anything like that before. I didn't even know cold existed like that. It was something completely new to me.

That was 2006. It was an experience for the whole two weeks I was there. My feet were cold the whole time. I didn't even warm up when I got back to Jamaica. My feet started peeling. There was all this dead skin. It was a good experience and I could share it with my family and other Jamaicans. I knew I was going back at some point, but I didn't know it would get colder. I thought that was the coldest it could get, but man I had a big surprise.

There was another guy named Devin Anderson and they sent him to the Yukon to train for the Yukon Quest. He went for a week or so and he came back to Jamaica and he said he wasn't going to do it. So they asked me. I didn't know the consequences. They said it would be a good opportunity, but they warned me, "You know it's going to be cold." I said, "Yeah, man."

I thought I knew the cold. They said, "You know it's going to be a one-thousand-mile dog-sled race." I said, "Yeah, man." I didn't know anything about a one-thousand-mile dog-sled race. I'd only been on a sled a couple of times in Minnesota. They said, "You're going to stay up there the whole winter, like five or six months." I said, "Yeah, man, no problem." They were going to spend a lot of money to take care of me and they didn't want me to change my mind. I think flying to the Yukon I had to take three different planes. We saw all of these mountains and the area was filled with ice. I thought, *What's up with the winter I know?*

In Jamaica, they don't mess around with cold at all, period. We were going to work with Hans Gatt and he met the plane with his girlfriend, Suzy. We ended up in Whitehorse. It was so cold in the Yukon it was painful. It was minus eighteen. Inside the tent was cold. I was just lost. I wondered what I had put myself into. It was so cold I wanted to go back to Jamaica.

But I stayed there and I ran the Yukon Quest in 2009. I finished thirteenth. I even won $4,000. That was supposed to be it, one time. But when I got back to Jamaica I thought about it. There are two big races and I only did one, so why not do the other one if I had the opportunity? I had more experience because I finished the Quest. On the other hand, there are twenty-four checkpoints in the Iditarod just in case. So I said, *Why not?*

That year [2010] I trained with Lance Mackey. I went to Fairbanks from Whitehorse. Those are just about the two coldest cities in North America, I think. I think it was September and I don't think there was any snow on the ground—yet. I knew what to expect from the cold, so that wasn't on my mind quite as much. I got to use a different team and the environment was more relaxed. I had more experienced dogs, too. So I did the Iditarod and as a rookie I finished forty-seventh.

So I did the Quest and the Iditarod and that meant I did both of the big races. If I did good I was not going to come back because this is foolishness. Then all of a sudden it hit me—*What did I mean about coming back?* You can't stop. The next two Iditarods I started, but I didn't finish. You always think you can do better.

People in Jamaica don't really follow cold-weather sports. I get some reaction that I am doing this from people who know about it. They are really excited for me, that a Jamaican can compete in something as great as this and as challenging. I did an interview on our TV station's morning show, *Smile Jamaica*. They had me on and they introduce me and they go, "Welcome. We have Newton 'Mad Man' Marshall." They called me that because they said only a mad man would go and do something as wicked as this. It was quite funny.

We talk about how cold it is as someone who has been through something like that and they say to me, "There's no way." Nobody can pay them to do that. Even if somebody was paying them, they wouldn't do it. Some Jamaicans understand the cold because they experienced it somewhere and have an idea. Most people just don't understand it unless you tell them or they have to go experience it for themselves. It is something new to Jamaicans, but some Jamaicans love the idea. They are glad that I am doing it and not them.

The first time I went to Minnesota was more than six years ago. I thought when I went to the Yukon it would be one time in a one-thousand-mile race, but here I am. Seriously, for me it was something new. I had never done any form of sports in my life, so it was completely new to me.

Dog mushing is something unique and I keep doing it, too, because none of my fellow Jamaicans are doing it. I'm the only one. I guess I have grown to love it over the years and I understand more what to do.

The first time I entered the Iditarod and was in Anchorage for the start it was all great for me. Having people cheer and wave and give me high-fives was great. I'm the only Jamaican so it was something special for me. The Iditarod fans knew who I was because I did the Yukon Quest. But some of them were still surprised: "Oh, there's a Jamaican on the trail. Whoa!" Along the trail some people even brought me a Red Stripe beer. Somebody ran up to me across the snow and tripping all over the place and he goes, "Here, Jamaica, have a Red Stripe." My word, I have never seen a big bottle of Red Stripe like that in my life. I don't know where they found it. It was huge.

Alaskans seem to like that I am here. I like the excitement. I love the fun. It's a serious race, but when I'm racing I want to have fun. I achieved my finish in the toughest race on earth, but I want to be happy while I'm doing it. I want to be happy deep down and not stress too much about it.

When I finished the Iditarod it was so special it is even hard for me to explain. It was huge. I felt tears coming out of my eyes. I felt it so deeply and then along the road people had the Jamaican flag. There was one Jamaican lady who was at the start and at the finish. She said she just couldn't leave without supporting the Jamaican dog-sled team. Coming into the finish she handed me a flag. I could hear reggae music coming from a building. It was just so great, the feeling of a lifetime that I can't forget. I will remember it forever. Fond memories.

Now I know many people in Alaska, too. People in Jamaica don't really know me. Nobody recognizes me because all they saw was a picture in the paper and I look like a big guy with a hood. They think I have lots of muscle. They got to know me a little bit in Alaska because I have kept coming back.

It's a good feeling, even in a checkpoint when I come into the villages it's great that there are people there to cheer for me, kids and all that. There's somebody different. It is such a pleasure to see different people, the Native people, the Eskimos. I always have fun. Even at the roughest times of my life, I always do.

The dogs have a good life, the best life anyone can live. They're warm. They get taken care of. They go out and run and then they get a ten-course meal. They get all kinds of meats and kibble.

I don't make a goal for finishing the Iditarod except to get to Nome. It depends on the dog team, how they run and the way they run. I want them to feel part of it as much as I want to feel part of it. We have to go together and if they're up to the challenge, then I'm up to the challenge. It depends on the bonding that we have. I know we can do something special. Special for me means being anywhere near the top. We'll just have to see what's out there for us.

I've been asked if I'm used to the cold yet, but I'm never going to get used to the cold. I think I can get used to the snow all of the time, but never the cold. I know it's something I can bear at minus ten or minus fifteen, but that's my point. I will work through whatever comes along, but that's the point where I feel comfortable running in.

Lower temperatures than that I feel my legs are getting numb. I've been in minus fifty-four on the trail. That's the coldest I've been in. That was in the Iditarod in 2010. I didn't know it was that cold at the time. I was wearing sealskin mittens and I stopped to put a bootie on a dog and I took the mitten off. When I went to put the mitten back on it was completely frozen. It was like a rock. I couldn't even get my hand back in it. I had to put my hand in my crotch to keep it warm. I couldn't leave it out. I didn't get frostbite. I'm glad.

It's so easy to get frostbite. I have had frostbite on my nose and on my cheeks. There is a lot of stuff you learn from mistakes you make and what you could have done better. You prepare yourself for the next race.

I was in Jamaica all during the summer [of 2013] and the temperature got over ninety degrees. My God, I was burning up. I don't think I lost any resistance to heat from being in Alaska. Eighty degrees for me is a normal thing. The summer before I was in Alaska and it got hot at times. People were complaining it was too hot, but I was just loving it. I just loved that nice warm weather in Alaska. When it got to be eighty degrees, it was just right for me. When you're in Jamaica and it's that hot, you get a lot of wind and there are a lot of trees. We have a mountain and it is always blowing off the mountain. I was born in the heat and that hasn't changed for me.

People have been very helpful to me, but I did not think I would be doing the Iditarod again and again. The only problem is raising money. This is an expensive sport. In Jamaica my salary for the year was like $3,000. I'm a security guard at a housing development now. I make $4,000. I could never do this, could never make it work out of my own pocket.

Up Hill Both Ways, painting, 2011.

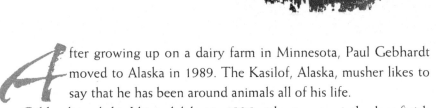

CHAPTER 23

Paul GEBHARDT

fter growing up on a dairy farm in Minnesota, Paul Gebhardt moved to Alaska in 1989. The Kasilof, Alaska, musher likes to say that he has been around animals all of his life.

Gebhardt made his Iditarod debut in 1996 with a twenty-sixth-place finish and only on rare occasions has he failed to finish in the top twenty. However, he did scratch once. In all, Gebhardt owns fourteen finishes in the top twenty.

The 2014 Iditarod was Gebhardt's eighteenth race. Twice, in 2000 and 2007, the fifty-eight-year-old musher finished second. Gebhardt has seven top-ten placings on his resume. There are sixty-five dogs in Gebhardt's Morning View Kennel on the Kenai Peninsula. Gebhardt's other profession is as a builder. He is a carpenter and contractor. He has also worked as a commercial fisherman. Besides being an avid hunter and fisherman, Gebhardt enjoys raising birds.

When I moved to Alaska from Minnesota in 1989 I met Dean Osmar, who had won the 1984 Iditarod. I bought a couple of sled dogs from him and I took them to Anvik where I was headed to build a lodge. Dean said whenever I got back to the Kenai he would have a job for me fishing. It didn't work out so well at the lodge and a month later I was back and got a job with Dean fishing.

I fished with Dean for seven years. During that same time period Martin Buser happened to be on Dean's crew, too, and we got paired up and became friends. I got my first puppies from Dean's bloodline and I helped Martin build his house in Big Lake. I worked off a stud fee from Martin's main stud dog, Dagger. That's how I got started with my first sled dogs. I got the female from Dean and crossbred them to Martin's line. I started my own line from there on.

Dean and Martin and I were all fishing. Commercial fishing takes a lot of upper body strength and there are stretches with no sleep, kind of like dog mushing. Those guys both kind of coaxed me into it. They said, "You should really race Iditarod. You'd be good at it. You could win." All that kind of stuff. I grew up on a farm and for my whole life I had been around animals. My family's dairy farm was about fifty miles west of Minneapolis. There was no dog mushing near us. Whatever mushing there was, it was way up north and I didn't go to that area except to hunt.

I love animals. I'd been around animals since I was born. The natural animal to have up here in Alaska is a sled dog. It worked out great for me and I still have eighty sled dogs. My dogs have done well for me over my career. We placed in the top five four times. I sold off my original main dogs in 2002 and came back and did the 2003 race with a new team of puppies all over again.

At the time I wanted to spend more time with my daughter. She was a senior in high school. What I did was save enough puppies to make another team. That's when I came back with a fresh team and placed twenty-third. Otherwise I've been in the top twenty all of the time. I've done well for myself with my own bloodline since that first litter with Dean and Martin. Time does fly. If you had asked me back then about looking ahead I would never have dreamt that I was going to be doing my eighteenth Iditarod. I would never have dreamt that ever. I still sometimes wonder why I sign up again, but I haven't won yet and it keeps driving me to go at it. As long as I'm competitive I'll probably keep racing just to try to win it.

I'm not sure if it's the sport and the racing that keeps me in the Iditarod or it's just as much the animals themselves. I'd say half of what I do with the sled dogs is me being able to breed, to raise up, to train, and sell my own bloodline. I'm pretty proud of what I created and I like to prove how good they are. You know, they're amongst the best.

Once I committed to my rookie year race I had no illusions I was going to win it or anything. I had a five-year project in mind. I decided right away that it would take a few years to get good at what I was doing. The thing I remember best about my rookie year was that was the year we sighted the polar bear on the West Coast. I was running with Tomas Israelsson, who was a friend of mine and still is to this day, Dewey Halverson, Diana Moroney, and Jerry Austin. I was running with a really good bunch of people. We all saw a polar bear and everybody told us we didn't because it couldn't be there. That was pretty impressive, a little hair-raising, but pretty impressive.

I had typical rookie feelings going on. I traveled with those guys and when I got to Koyuk I had probably the fastest team out of all of them. We were going to take a six-hour rest and then leave. I felt whipped. I got up to leave with those guys and I said, "You know, my dogs look really, really tired. They need more rest." They said, "No, they don't. No, they don't." Being a veteran now I recognize that they didn't, but I thought so, and so I stayed six hours more at Koyuk, which is 175 miles from the finish line. After twelve hours, the checkers told me I needed to leave.

My dogs were stirring around. I got going and I passed Diana right by the gold dredge by Nome and I could see Tomas and Dewey in front of me. So I made up that whole six hours. But what sticks in my mind is that the dog team really wasn't that tired, it was me that was tired and not knowing how to deal with that. It didn't take long for me to start learning how to deal with that fatigue. That's why you don't see rookies winning this no matter how good they are.

What I tell people—and I introduce a lot of people to mushing and explain what it's all about—is that I never stop learning on a race. Just when I think I've seen it all, I see something new. When I quit learning things at races, I'll probably quit doing this. But that will never happen. You'll always learn something if you pay attention. As long as you read your animals you will learn something.

I talk to Dean Osmar all the time. I live across the street. We always talk about who is going to win this thing and the different teams that are capable of winning it. There are so many teams that are capable of winning it now. That has changed a lot. We say it's 25 percent dog team, 25 percent musher, and 50 percent luck and weather. From the first Iditarod I did till now, when I started racing by the time you got to Takotna there were fifteen or twenty teams, and that was your top twenty. Now you get to Takotna and there are forty-six teams out there that are going to try to be your top twenty. That's how many good teams there are and they don't stop dropping off that fast like they used to. They used to spread out.

In 2013, there were twenty-seven teams into White Mountain when Mitch [Seavey] crossed the finish line. That never happened like that. If you're in the top ten, you can win. That's the way I feel. It is good breeding and the modern-day mushers aren't like the old days when the top mushers used to keep a lot of secrets. Everything's pretty much out in the open. Everybody shares everything. The breeding program has gotten better. We're breeding better dogs. The food, the nutrition's, gotten tremendously better, and the dog care has gotten tremendously better. The dog care getting better I attribute to the veteran mushers not keeping secrets from what will make a dog better.

It used to be when I first started you couldn't get them to tell you squat. By us teaching the younger mushers, the newer group is learning what the dogs are really capable of as long as you take care of them. There's very, very few outstanding, super dogs anymore like there was a Granite [Susan Butcher's leader], like there was Andy [Rick Swenson's leader]. My lead dog, Red Dog, was a phenomenal leader. Red Dog in his background had Granite, he had Andy, he had Dagger, Martin's main stud when he started winning. That trickled down into mine. Red Dog didn't need to sleep. I still have pictures of him in Unalakleet sitting while the rest of my team lies down to sleep. I've been waiting the rest of my life to find another dog like that and I probably won't.

The thing is that the dogs have improved. You're not seeing the record in the Iditarod being broken by leaps and bounds anymore. We're just playing with that. We haven't reached as fast as it can go, but we're not going to go that much faster. I've seen a lot of ways the Iditarod has been run. Run six hours, rest six hours. Run four hours, rest four hours. Run eight hours, rest four hours. And go farther to take your twenty-four-hour mandatory rest. I was one of those. I went to Galena. Martin tried to run all of the way to

Rohn and that didn't work out. Things don't always pan out. Something different will work, but who knows what it is at this point?

Lance Mackey and I proved in 2007 when we finished first and second that you can run a longer distance and rest less. Lance and I traveled together that first victory he got. I was the one who came up with the plan. If you look at the times you're finishing with now, we're still finishing in nine days and six hours, the same times Martin Buser did, and Doug Swingley [the four-time champion] did, and I did when I took second by a long shot. We're not getting much faster. The distance is the same. Somewhere in there you're going to see people going back to the running faster and resting more again. It is gonna happen.

Then people will think we've got to get faster dogs again. They tried that with the hounds and then they got too much hound. Then they faded away from the hounds. It's fascinating to watch. It'll never stop improving. It's fun.

The biggest thing I had happen to me on the trail was in 2006, when I lost my whole team into Farewell Burn when I hit a tree. That was the year I went to Galena to take my twenty-four. I was towards the front. I left Rohn. There were about eight or ten mushers. I had built this great big sled. It had a seven-foot bed. It was full of food and a bale of straw on top. I was going to camp. Unfortunately, when you build a big sled like that and you weight it down, they don't steer worth a hoot.

This is at night, like four in the morning, the only one left ahead of me is Doug Swingley. We're coming up just about to Farewell Lake and I passed Swingley—he was camping. I go, *All right, I'm in the lead in the Iditarod.* There was a spruce tree, about four inches in diameter right off the side of the trail and my sled did not turn and it ran smack-dab into the middle of that spruce tree. I came to a sudden stop. I hung on to the handlebars and I flew over the handlebars and landed in my sled. I heard this crack. My gang-line broke right at the carabiner where it attaches to the sled. I jumped out of the sled and the dogs started trotting off across the lake. Fifteen of them I had yet. I'm running behind them going, "Whoa, whoa." They get faster and faster. I yelled, "Gee" and "Haw" trying to run them into the bushes. But they're on this lake and they got away from me.

So I started walking. My sled is off to the side of the trail. Now it's like six o'clock in the morning, just getting light. I pull off my jacket and I hang it on a tree because I'm sweating now because I'm trotting fast. I put my hat on a tree. I put my mittens on a tree. I'm just after my dog team. It was in the twenties, above zero, so it was really hot. It's fifty miles to Nikolai and there is not one more dog team between me and Nikolai that can stop these guys so they're going to run all of the way to Nikolai or get tangled up or kill themselves. Bad things happen with a loose dog team.

All of a sudden, behind me comes Doug Swingley. "Hop on the sled," he said, and I hopped on his sled. He gave me a ride and I kind of explained what happened. I thought we would never catch them with me as extra weight on his sled. I knew he had a fast team, but not that fast. We went about two miles and there was a buffalo hunter's camp with a snowmobile there. I said, "I'm stealing that snowmobile." I jumped off his sled and I told him if he catches them just to tangle them up.

The hunters were still sleeping and I hollered in their tent, "I'm taking your snowmobile" and they're going, "What? What?" I said, "I'm in the Iditarod and my dog team's on the loose and I got to go catch them." They said, "Go ahead." I race off as fast as I can and then I see one dog curled up in the middle of the trail. It was my wheel dog, my slowest one, who had slipped her harness and got left behind. It took me forty-five minutes to catch the dog team in the rolling hills.

I pulled up alongside of them and Governor—he was one of my really, really good leaders—and he looked at me. They were just loping along and he had a smile on his face. I said, "Whoa" and they came to a halt. They all stop and I tied the dogs off single file. I met Doug and told him everything was OK. I'm meeting all of these different mushers and they're going, "Are you OK? Are you OK?" I got all of the way back to the buffalo hunters, and I got hooked up to the sled. I'm trying not to interfere with any musher.

John Barron pulls up next to me and my sled is hooked up to a snowmobile to get me back to the dogs and he stares at me. I go, "Goddamn, this is way faster." Then I explained to him what happened. He said, "Go ahead of me and just catch up to your dog team." I got 'em back. It took me over four hours. Then I had to stand out there and remake my whole gangline and put all of my dogs back in harness. So the mushers are going by me and I've got dogs tied off in the bushes. One dog tied here and one dog tied there. And I had to go to the bathroom, so I go behind this tree. I'm going to the bathroom and here comes Lance Mackey and we had trained together because he lived right next to me [before moving to Fairbanks]. He can't see me and he's looking at all my dogs spread out everywhere.

I got into Nikolai and I tell my story to Mark Nordman (the race marshal) and Lance hears it. He goes, "What a relief. I was trying to figure out your new strategy on how to rest a dog team." The whole thing turned out pretty good. I finished third. It was quite an episode. That's probably the most memorable moment I'll ever have in Iditarod. You go from the lowest lows to the highest highs. I took my twenty-four in Galena and I left there in seventeenth place and a hundred miles later I was in fourth. The dogs were just flying. I still had fifteen into Shaktoolik. It was a fun race, with an interruption.

CHAPTER 24

DeeDee
JONROWE

One of the most popular of Iditarod racers and a longtime competitor, DeeDee Jonrowe of Willow, Alaska, is one of a small number of mushers who have been involved in the sport full-time over a period of decades and have made it their livelihood.

Jonrowe, sixty, is a graduate of the University of Alaska Fairbanks and has been mushing since 1979. Husband Mike, who always helps Jonrowe train the dogs in their kennel, is a commercial fisherman by trade. In 2014 Jonrowe competed in her thirty-second Iditarod.

Although she has never won the championship Jonrowe has twice finished second, in 1993 and 1998. She owns fifteen top-ten finishes.

Jonrowe has twice won the Humanitarian Award, twice won the Most Inspirational Musher Award, and also won the Sportsmanship Award. Active in fund-raising for charities and known for her strong religious commitment, Jonrowe has coped with and conquered breast cancer.

The veteran musher also owns nine Iditarod finishes in under ten days for the one-thousand-mile event. The 2014 race, however, was perhaps her most frustrating. Jonrowe's team was caught up in the worst of the horrible early race trail and the resulting crash dumped her from the sled, forcing her to scratch two days into the event.

My first Iditarod was in 1980 after I started running dogs in 1979 when I lived in Bethel. I don't think I ever would have imagined I would still be running dogs in 2014. I don't know if I could even have visualized 2014.

You can't stop if you're going to stay competitive. People who take a year or two off don't usually come back and do very well. Jeff King came back to a scratch and then to a good finish, but it's unusual to take any time off and stay competitive. The margins are so thin compared to the early days. Then, just good kibble could make the difference of a day. A day, not an hour, much less a plastic sled or Velcro booties compared to taping them on. That was a huge jump, a big time saver. Those are some examples of things that changed in a big way.

You look at drivers like Linwood Fiedler and Joe Garnie, some of the guys, good drivers, who try to take time off and they can't ever get back in the saddle. The race just rushes by them in a thunderbolt and they just can't catch up.

Dog mushing is my career. And there was no such thing as this career when I started. Martin Buser and I talked about that. We are among the first to have this career. We developed the professional long-distance driver with the kennels and year-around program speaking, and all of the other pieces of the puzzle that go with being able to be a full-time musher, raising pups, training year-round, using dogs on a glacier. There was no such thing and there was no place to go and mentor somebody. There were no handlers, except a kennel partner that helped you run dogs, or a neighbor or family member. There was no concept of somebody coming and spending a winter with you as a handler.

When I started out it was kids making booties from patterns that you bought from somebody in town and equipment was whatever kind you could find or having somebody making it when they could. Most of the stuff wasn't available for sale. You were always looking for somebody who could sew. I never had time to stop and really get into sewing. I was busy fishing for my dogs—that was state-of-the-art food in rural Alaska. That's when I was in Bethel. When I moved to Willow I worked as a fishing guide for Mahays on the Talkeetna River. I worked in Bristol Bay for years and all of the way down to Ketchikan buying fish as a fish company representative. My degree is in biological sciences and renewable resources from the University of Alaska Fairbanks.

A lot of the things I learned in college were useful, from genetics to nutrition. A lot of the biology things were useful. There were a lot of things that are applicable to being at the top of your game as something as a survivalist in mushing. That's the cool thing about the sport. It has so many moving parts. It's a huge chess game.

I've never been the one to make big technological advances. Equipment has never really fascinated me. I want it to work for me and that's about as much fascination as I have, whereas some of the guys technology has really caught their eye and they've really progressed the sport because of the technological advances they've brought to it. That wasn't my specialty. My specialty was nutrition, care. Mine was all about the dogs, all about the heartbeat. I'm an animal lover. I shared my life with lots of animals, whether they're sled dogs, Labradors, Pekinese, or kitty cats, moose calves, fish. Anything that has a heartbeat has always fascinated me.

Consequently, one of the things I enjoy is studying behavior of any kind of animal or bird. One of the things that brought me to the Delta was that I was studying waterfowl, the waterfowl coming in, and nesting, and then going to Cordova and watching the spring migration come in. I did those things as a college student long before I ever thought I was going to be running dogs.

When I started in the Iditarod the sport was young. It's not the same as horse racing when times have not changed or come down for twenty years or so. There are not as many pieces of the puzzle to be tweaked in thoroughbred racing as there are in dog mushing. One event happens over a few minutes as opposed to an event that happens over days and one event happens on a contained track while the other one takes you across the Arctic. There are huge variables involved such as climate changes and trail changes.

There has never been an earthquake that changed the Kentucky Derby track, yet there was an earthquake that took half a mountain down right outside of the Post River and changed our trail significantly in one movement. We get a wilderness fire and it changes our ability to travel across that piece of ground for years.

Genetically, I'm not sure if our dogs are getting faster. I think there will come a finite point of how fast a dog can be. But we've learned to take care of them better. It's like we've been able to take human Olympic advances and put them together with canine medicine. There has been a fascination with the canine world nutritionally. A lot of the canine dog food companies, the nutritional experts from Paris to Ohio and Indiana, are all intrigued, so they've brought forty years of interesting science to the table as they learn how to provide better, more absorbable, faster recovery for our dogs. So they seem faster because they recover faster because they never got as down to start with.

We get to Nome faster because the dogs can recover. In my first Iditarod I finished in twenty-fourth place and it took more than seventeen days. In my fastest Iditarod it took nine days and eight hours. Nutrition is not all of it, but it's a major component.

In 1980, when Martin and I were rookies, one of the best things you could do was to pull into a village and ask if there was any freshly trapped beaver. Then you would buy that carcass from the trapper and chop it up and give it to the dogs. That was the top-of-the-art thing in nutrition. Imagine how long it took for a dog to metabolically turn that into fuel as opposed to some of the foods we have now that we provide them with every two hours as they travel down the trail. Their blood levels and their nutritional levels never cave because we're providing something for them constantly. We understand them better. Same with the way we use booties. We used to put booties on a dog if it had a bad foot. Now you see full teams of dogs booted up at all times because it's better for them. They run faster.

It's not just treatment, it is prevention. I had no idea what a chiropractor was until I moved onto the road system, much less a chiropractic adjustment for a dog. Acupuncture is the same thing. I never had a massage until I moved onto the road system, I guarantee you that. I didn't realize the concept of a sports massage for aching muscles. And we apply those to our canine athletes and that has made our times faster.

It's remarkable to me how much faster we go, but I can't spend too much time pondering the past or I'll be in the past. I've watched the race leave some guys alongside the trail. They're dwelling too much on the good old days and I have to be thinking about Dallas Seavey, the future days, the young up-and-comers. I can't rest on the past until I've decided to live in the past. That would be retirement.

We had great races in the 1990s when six or seven of us could break loose from the pack and we were racing for the top five. The rest of the pack was too far behind to get us and that was great because it took the pressure off. A lot of times you knew you were going to do well.

One of my favorite races was in 2012 when I had sixteen dogs and I didn't drop my first dog until Cripple. I dropped my first dogs in 2013 in Iditarod because they were in heat. I was traveling competitively and racing hard with a beautiful dog team and I felt everything was coming together for me. I'm so fortunate to still be in the game and still think that at any point I can break loose and grab that lead.

Now there are maybe twenty teams that can run up front, not just five or six of us. What has happened is mentoring—these mushers are the kids of competitive mushers or were the handlers for them. They didn't develop their own bloodlines. Their bloodlines were already developed. They didn't have to develop the equipment. They didn't have to develop the food. All of those things were in place for them. They worked for competitive teams for a couple of years. They got littermates of those guys' teams and instantly they ran the race. They had state-of-the-art gear, nutrition, and dogs. They were young with state-of-the-art things. They have GPS systems and computers and throw all of the numbers together and it just comes down to their motivation. They didn't have judgment because you can't buy judgment. And experience can be incredibly important on the trail, especially if there are storms.

My experience helps me make good decisions. That's one thing I always feel good about. You know all of the good and you know all of the bad. It might make you more cautious. That could hold you back in one of those just-throw-caution-to-the-wind moves. If that's the case, so be it because I have to come home and look my dogs in the eyes and know I did right by them. I've done that for thirty-five years and I've learned to be at peace with my performance.

The Iditarod is more than a competition to me. It's a lifestyle, but it's also a training ground for the deep, dark, hard things in life. It's been a place to test my faith. It's tested my strength and my judgment and my resolve and all of those things came into play when I was in a serious car accident, when I was going through cancer, when I was taking my mom through cancer, and most recently the hardest thing I've done is to take care of my dad until he died from cancer. The hardest thing I've ever had happen is when my father was in hospice and I was the primary caregiver. That was horrible. It was a labor of love and resolve and the Iditarod trained me.

There have been hard times on the trail and quitting wasn't an option. I couldn't say to my father, "Dad, this is too hard, I can't do it." On the trail I couldn't do it to me and I couldn't do it to my dogs. I couldn't just give up. That did not change the circumstances. It doesn't change your reality. But the Iditarod has taught me over and over again not to give up. I look forward to those challenges whatever they are. You never know what they are going to be.

I never expected forty-two degrees and rain, but the hardest thing has been dead cold, a windchill of minus one hundred, with a headwind. That's cold. You're in survival mode taking care of the dogs and yourself. Some years I've done a better job, but one of the worst jobs I did was in 2002 when I ended up in the hospital in Nome. I got dehydrated in Golovin Bay and that was the year I was diagnosed with breast cancer. I had health issues. I was in five different hospitals that year. That wasn't a good year.

But better years came. That's one thing when you have longevity in the race. You have bad years, but better years come. In 2012 and 2013 I felt really good and I thought it was pretty good to be ten years older and feel that much better than I had ten years ago. That kind of gift comes from cancer and recovery. I knew there was something major wrong. People were telling me I was just getting older and I said, "I didn't get this old this fast."

One funny thing from the perspective of being older and around the Iditarod a long time is that some of the young drivers are just babies behavior-wise. They want to know where they can plug in their rechargeable batteries. Are there extra outlets? Can we get more extension cords? Their GPS has got to be charged. They've got to recharge their GPS. Coming into Rohn somebody wants to know if they can recharge their iPad. "There's no microwave in the checkpoint. How am I going to thaw my food? I don't have anything to eat because there's no microwave."

I look at (veteran) Sonny Lindner and we roll our eyes. I'm going, *Get a life! I don't even know if I can stay in the cabin with you.* I think, *Where's your reality?* That's not the image of the Iditarod. Those kinds of things make me go, "Arrgh!"

One thing that dog mushers do that is different from other professional athletes is spend so much time out there encouraging young people, supporting causes. Mushers are athletes who get out making appearances in fund drives for kids that have special needs. They're involved in Special Olympics. I'm going to Unalakleet for a Blueberry Festival 5K. I'm going to Fairbanks to talk to Fort Yukon School District teachers. I did some stuff encouraging kids to read and I wasn't the only one.

Other professional athletes in basketball, baseball, and football are much more highly paid. Only a small percentage of mushers are even professionals. Nobody ever got rich doing the Iditarod. You've got to have supplemental sources of income, a half a dozen of them maybe, entrepreneurial things they bring to the table. Nonetheless mushers are out there in schools talking to young people, doing things in their communities.

The Iditarod has changed a lot since I began racing. It has grown and it has gained much more awareness Outside. One huge thing is the Teacher on the Trail program and how teachers and their classrooms follow the race in schools all over the country. My mom, Peg Stout, drew up the first curriculum. That program has exploded.

There are sponsors who bring a teacher to Alaska to follow the race every year and they vie for it. It's like a scholarship that a teacher gets. They submit elaborate programs, everything from physical fitness programs to mathematical programs to science programs and computerized programs. Those curriculums are sold all over the world now. Then there's teleconferencing. It's absolutely exploded.

There was a time when I used to travel that I had to explain what the Iditarod was. People asked, "What's the Iditarod?" Now people know what it is. They may not understand all of the concepts of it, but they know it's a long race in the winter in Alaska. That it's a great adventure.

The Iditarod is never the same. You don't have the same dog team. It isn't the same trail. There aren't the same trail conditions. And to be honest, if I'm any example, you're never the same. Things have happened to define the musher differently. Maybe I'm better. Maybe things are tougher. Maybe I'm more resolved. Maybe I'm more distracted. There's always something that has changed. It's the kind of competition that takes such single-minded focus, but every year you're a different competitor.

They say that the most difficult thing to do is to repeat a championship and that's why. That's exactly the concept, that people change, or things happen. That's one reason it is so phenomenal what Lance Mackey did, winning the Iditarod four years in a row—and two different long-distance races four times. Year after year. I haven't done the Yukon Quest yet. It's still out there. Still a goal yet unfulfilled. It just hasn't worked out yet.

Right now the focus of my life is my family and my mother has needed me. I won't do another one-thousand-mile race in the same year as the Iditarod as long as she needs me. My dad [Ken Stout], who passed away last year, needed me, too. It reminds me how short time can be. It's Mom and Mike and if I had to make choices dog racing would go to the back of the pack.

That affected my fall schedule. The prognosis on Dad wasn't good. He had six months to two years and he had a few things he wanted to do. Mom and Dad and I and my sister Linda and Mike went to Missouri. Dad wanted to relive all his memories with us. He showed us where our grandparents are buried, where he was born, where he and Mom dated. For two weeks we ran around the Springfield, Missouri, area meeting all his old friends.

We did all this stuff that was Dad's fun. Dad just had a blast and I saw the clock ticking, ticking, ticking until the end of September. I didn't start running dogs until the end of September and I reminded myself I couldn't be worried about that. Dad was the important thing. I was thinking it was probably going to be the only fall I would do this with him. I had a tenth-place finish and the training didn't matter because it was the same as the tenth-place finish from the year before. It was a different set of dogs, a different set of circumstances. I'm so pleased that I understood that Dad was the focus and thankful that Mike supported me in it.

Last year Mike was fishing in Bristol Bay for two months and he got right off the boat and flew to Springfield. Mom had her heart set on driving up the highway, so Mike drove her in five days. I think that's pretty amazing that right after he got off the boat he brought his mother-in-law up the Alaska Highway like that.

I have been a fishing guide on the Talkeetna River and done other things in the summer for jobs, but I went to work doing tour groups with Martin Buser in 2013. There were buses of people. Some of them came off cruises and some are their own tours. Martin has a really nice operation set up and he's building a visitors center that will make it even nicer. Martin and his son Rohn and I do the presentations and Kathy, Martin's wife, does all the scheduling. It's great fun. I love it.

Usually the visitors know who I am. Either because their tour guide told them about me or they've seen an Iditarod DVD, or they follow the race.

We're able to give them a lot of stories and answer their questions. I enjoy it. People are interested. The slowest day of the week was ninety-three people. There are a lot of people interested and most of them are dog lovers. You should see them when we pull the puppies out. We talk about the dogs, and that's the focus of Martin's presentation. That's one reason why I enjoy working his tour so much. We talk about the evolution of Alaska huskies, where they came from, and how they are a working race team. It's not Balto or *Snow Dogs* or big puppies. We talk about how they're bred and what we look for. People think the dogs should be bigger.

We educate them about Iditarod dogs. They understand when you give them the explanation about the kind of endurance athletes these dogs are as opposed to strength athletes that some of the bulkier, heavier dogs are. Then they understand that correlation. Then we hook the dogs up, seven dogs, for an exhibit, and Rohn runs on a sled with steel runners. The dogs are their own best advocates. They hug you like coworkers. They go to work with great eagerness.

The tourists can see how great the dogs are. Martin and I have the same philosophy with our dogs and it's easy for us to work together and tell stories. I enjoy it.

I still think I can win. My motivation for doing the Iditarod might morph as time goes by, but my motivation for quitting will always be the same and that will be when I don't think I can keep my dog team safe. When I present a danger to the safety of my team, that's when I need to consider stepping off the runners.

Right now I still go into the race thinking this one could be the one I win. I have the team and the backing, so I do believe that.

Puppy Love, official Iditarod poster, 2003.

CHAPTER 25

Mike WILLIAMS JR.

*M*ike Williams Jr. is following in the footsteps of his father, longtime Iditarod competitor Mike Williams Sr. The younger Williams is now the main man in the kennel out of the family's home base in Akiak, a small village of a few hundred people in Southwest Alaska.

Recently married and the father of twin boys, Williams, twenty-nine, made his Iditarod debut in 2010 and has competed in five races. He has made a splash with some high finishes, including eighth place in 2012. Williams has long helped his dad prepare their huskies for races, so it was natural to ease into the main musher mode a few years ago when Mike Sr. turned sixty. Mike Jr. had been the main handler in the dog yard for years.

An accomplished carpenter who built his own house across the street from his parents' house, Mike Jr. spends part of his summers working construction when he can, but he is also involved in commercial fishing inseason and catches fish to feed the dogs in his lot.

Considered one of the most promising mushers in the younger generation moving up, Williams said he has been around dogs since he was born.

I kind of grew up in the dog yard. We always had dogs and every summer the dogs had puppies and being a kid I liked playing with the puppies. I also remember bundling up in one of my dad's parkas and curling up in the sled for a ride on one of his training runs.

Pretty soon being around the dogs I wanted to race. I started off training puppies when I was in the second or third grade. I took out four dogs at a time. Then by sixth grade, or junior high, I started taking out up to eight dogs. I was just taking them out for runs. They weren't the dogs training for the Iditarod. I ran the puppies. Sometimes I ran them as early as five months old.

Both the puppies and I were gaining experience together. I wouldn't always run them with a trained leader and this was with the puppies running for the first time. They were running in harness without a leader and that was a crazy ride. Sometimes I would make a lucky pick on two dogs and they would take off in front like they'd been running their whole life.

I found out early on that I liked to race. We had local races where I ran one dog. I couldn't wait for the winter dog races. The biggest race around here for us is the Kuskokwim 300 in Bethel. That's very close by and that's the biggest middle-distance race. I think the first time I ran that I was twenty-one. I had done some smaller races before that. After high school I went to Seward for a year and attended the Alaska Vocational Technical Center and learned to be a carpenter. I have worked on construction in the summers and I built my family's house.

We had trained to do the Kusko and I had a really good team, but on the homestretch to Bethel I injured a couple of dogs. There were some snow-drifts. The snow was higher than usual that year and I knew I had them running at a good pace and that it could be a risk, but my dogs were moving and I let them run. Outside of Akiak there was a snowdrift and I didn't hit the brake in time. I think my leader stepped in a little crack and she sprained her wrist and the dog behind her got a muscle strain on his shoulder. I wasn't aware of it at first. I loaded the leader into the sled and switched leaders and then passing Akiak I noticed the second dog had a problem and I had to put two dogs in the sled. That took a lot of time. I didn't finish as well as I had hoped, but I'm pretty sure that I got on the minds of some of the mushers.

Although I had wanted to do the Iditarod for some time I didn't know when I was going to be able to. My dad was always telling me to help him train and when he went off to do the Iditarod I stayed home with the dogs left behind and ran the little races.

My first Iditarod in 2010 I finished twenty-sixth. I actually slept good the night before the race. I wasn't too nervous about the trail. I was nervous about trying to stay awake. That's probably one of the biggest challenges, taking care of yourself and the dogs. I was happy to finish. For me twenty-sixth was kind of high for my first run and after the race I was thinking about it and how much more I can improve.

I knew I could do this differently and training I knew I could differently. I could do more mileage and get them more prepared. It's a tough race and they make a lot of longer runs with shorter rests than they used to. Each year you pick up a storehouse of knowledge, especially for training and taking care of the dogs, and how to choose which ones will make it and which ones won't.

My first race I finished in ten days and six hours. My second race was much faster. In 2011 I finished thirteenth in nine days and twelve hours. The dogs were much better trained for it. I kind of had a hard time, though. My dogs got diarrhea and got skinny. They got skinnier before I knew it. They were fast, but they were a little bit leaner than most at the start. My thinking was that they were marathon runners and when you see human marathon runners you're not going to see fat on them. I had in mind that as long as I kept feeding and feeding them, snacking them, and they got in their calories, then they would be fine. I didn't think about them getting sick.

It was kind of humiliating because the vets were kind of on me about it. They kept saying to feed my dogs and I kept telling them I was feeding them. "Look at their stomachs. Look at their place in the race." I'd stop and feed them two full buckets of food. One of the mushers came over and said, "Holy cow. Your dogs don't look bad. They're kind of lean, but they don't look bad. They're eating a lot better than mine." They were all on their feet and going after their food. They got stronger as we went on and I had one of the fastest times from Kaltag to Nome, from Unalakleet to Nome.

At one point I was running in the top five and in the middle of the race in the top ten, but when I started giving the dogs more rest people started passing me. Then I went back to doing shorter rests and passed a lot of them back.

When I finished thirteenth and saw my time I was content with that. I looked at the times in Unalakleet and I think I was eighteenth, so I passed a lot of those guys from Unalakleet to White Mountain, and I passed a couple more from White Mountain to Nome. So I felt pretty good about the run and the dogs bounced back.

There's no question that the Iditarod is different every year. People always run some different dogs that have never run before. Dogs can get sick. The weather changes. In that 2010 race the first part of it from Willow to Rainy Pass was all smooth. The trail was soft and the snow was so high on the sides it was like the dogs were running in a tunnel. Then in some places snowdrifts were blown over.

Dogs have always been in our family. My dad always had dogs and our people always had dogs. My Uncle Walter was a pretty big racer around here. Then my Uncle Willie was a pretty good racer and dog driver. When I did my first Iditarod I knew a few mushers already, but some of them asked, "Who are you?" They said they didn't recognize me. Definitely my first year. But so many people come up to me and mention my dad and ask how he's doing and to tell him they said hi. I can't keep track of all of them.

When I placed eighth I guess I had in mind from the year before to be a little bit more careful. I had made the mistake of not feeding them enough fat in training and then all of a sudden I gave them a pretty good amount and I think that's why they got sick. In 2012 I didn't have as much of a problem. I was just doing my own thing. I wasn't too worried about chasing after other teams. Of course, before the race you have a plan that we want to do, but plans change. I just kept thinking, *I'm just going to go and do what's best by my dogs.* It felt like they were getting stronger and stronger.

In 2012, I was happy. I was right there with Mitch Seavey. After the race he told me he thought I was John Baker, but I caught John alongside of Cape Nome and passed him there. My parents were there at the finish. I think they were proud of me. Breaking into the top ten is not an easy thing to do, especially with the competition today. All of the races are really close from first place to tenth place, just a few hours' difference.

It made me think what I can do in the future. As a competitor you want to win and I think I can do it. I think I can. In fact, I know I can do it. But you still have to learn as you go.

In 2013 both me and my dad ran the race. That may be the only time that happens. It was good to see him out there. We were going along together, but at the checkpoints he was telling me to go. I'd roll up and stay a couple of hours and he woke me up and said, "Get up. It's time to go." He said, "All those guys are going. You need to go." I said, "I'm going to rest another hour." I finished twenty-sixth and he finished forty-fifth.

I was telling him that my dogs needed a little bit more rest. It was the type of training they did. I did a lot of ten- to twenty-mile runs and then I jumped them up to longer runs. I had in my mind that it was training to be up with the frontrunners. After 2013 my goal was to get back up near the front. I had a bunch of young dogs when I finished eighth. Now they are in their prime, four years old and five years old. They're pretty tough-minded.

I've always been known around Akiak and Bethel, but I wasn't that known statewide. The villages are small and everybody knows everybody. Then more people get to know you from the race. I get mail from around the Lower 48 now. It's mostly from students and it comes from school projects where they tell the students to pick a musher and write to them. Sometimes I get letters from them when I am still on the trail. I read the letters after I come back home. They were cheering me on. They say things like, "The last time I checked you were in Kaltag and you were doing really well. Go get 'em. I hope you win." Stuff like that. They're mostly from kids. They come from Illinois, New Jersey, all over. There are some from Jamaicans and Brazilians.

I don't really think about it too much that people know me in those places. I just know that I'm going to be doing the Iditarod and that I can only do the best I can do. There is a lot of work and time that goes into it. I don't want to do it just to get to the finish line. I want to give it my best. Yep, but the goal is always to win.

CHAPTER 26

Pete
KAISER

A rural Alaskan who grew up in Bethel, Pete Kaiser comes from a family that has long run dogs and he began his own mushing career as a youth. Like his friend from the area, Mike Williams Jr., Kaiser has dogs in his blood and began racing as a youngster. The two pals have been racing against one another in local races for years.

Kaiser, twenty-seven, made his Iditarod debut in 2010 with a twenty-eighth-place finish. Since then he swiftly blossomed into a top-tier competitor who posted top-ten placings. Almost overnight, Kaiser became a championship contender, finishing eighth in 2011 and fifth in 2012 before a thirteenth-place finish in 2013.

An employee of Knik Construction/Bering Marine, Kaiser spent time after high school graduation sampling course offerings at the University of Alaska Fairbanks and the University of Alaska Anchorage at his parents' urging, but preferred a more outdoorsy lifestyle and threw himself into mushing.

Laughingly, Kaiser explained how the number of dogs in the family kennel multiplied as if they were rabbits. Growing up watching the Kuskokwim 300, the most prestigious middle-distance race, in his own backyard, inspired Kaiser to make his start and led to his desire to compete in the Iditarod.

I was pretty much born into sled dogs. My father, Ron, had dogs, but he sold out to focus on family. When I was about five or six I got a husky dog as a pet. Then we got two or three more and it turned into five. Suddenly, it was that we only needed three or four more for a team. Pretty soon the group was ten or fifteen dogs and we had a small kennel.

My sister Tillie, who is three years younger, and I, enjoyed the dogs so our family got back into mushing. It was not to race, but just for fun and to do camping trips. In high school, between classes and sports, I didn't have a ton of time to spend with the dogs. But in 2003 I raced in the Akiak Dash, which is sixty-five miles long. I was a sophomore in high school. I was fourth or something like that. It's kind of a big deal around here.

In 2005 I won it. We weren't really expecting to win. I took the lead within a mile of the mass start. I won $3,000 and I thought, *How can I do this better?* I did the Bogus Creek 150 that year and I graduated from high school in the spring. The Bogus Creek is from Bethel and back and it is a big-time mid-distance race for local mushers along with the Kusko. I have a framed picture hanging on the wall in a hallway of me and my dogs. Then I got a video of the 2005 Iditarod and I watched it like one thousand times.

After I finished high school I put college on the back burner for a little while, but I had committed to starting school at UAF in January of 2006. The timing was perfect. The Bogus Creek race was scheduled to start and a day or two later school was going to start. But then there was severe windchill and the start of the race was postponed. My parents were adamant that I couldn't miss the first day of school. So I couldn't race and my dad ran the team. I was so mad we didn't talk for a while.

The whole time I was at school all I could think of was dogs, dogs, dogs. Then I switched to UAA. In January 2007—my dad must have trained the dogs till then—I came home at Christmas break and I was able to train the dogs for a month and I took second in the Bogus Creek. Then I was pretty much hooked.

I went back to school and it was just another miserable winter of wanting to be running dogs. I had pretty much decided, *This is what I want. I'm going to give it a shot.* The next year I stayed home from school and trained and in

January of 2008 I won the Bogus Creek 150. Going into the race I felt like I had a pretty good shot. It was pretty cool.

After that I didn't go back to college. My parents handled that pretty well. They've been super supportive. I think they realized quickly that I wasn't just doing the mushing for fun and I was pretty serious about it. For me it was eat, sleep, breathe mushing.

In 2009 I entered the Kuskokwim 300. That was a childhood dream. There are a lot of big-name mushers who come to Bethel for that. Mitch Seavey won and I came in sixth. I won the Rookie of the Year Award. I felt good. I was racing with guys like Martin Buser, Jeff King, and John Baker. It was funner than hell, but looking back I didn't know anything about what I was doing.

I went into the Kusko thinking that I just wanted to finish. The Kusko was probably a turning point for me when I did that well. When I finished that high it felt as if the hard work had definitely paid off. I started to think, *This could turn into a career.*

That was my first big year of racing. I did the Tustemena 200, which was two weeks after the Kusko, and the Kobuk 440, too. I got my qualifying races done for the Iditarod. All went well, so that's when I decided to do the Iditarod. I first got the idea that I might want to do the Iditarod when I was in high school. It had been in the back of my mind. I thought it would be cool to do the Iditarod. It wasn't until later, after doing the middle-distance races, that I really considered doing it. I didn't even know I had a team that could compete. But Ed Iten, the Iditarod musher from Kotzebue, he used to stay with us for the Kusko and I picked his brain.

Given the group of mushers I was competing against, to finish sixth in the Kusko was a big deal for me. I was running dogs that I didn't even think made up a special team. My thinking was, *Wow, look at what I did and this team isn't even what I consider to be a good team.* It was a motley crew. The team was made up mainly of dogs that other people didn't want. They were good dogs, though.

I have been at the start of every Kusko for more than twenty years. It got started around the time I was born. When I ran the Kusko I thought, *You might as well go to the Iditarod.* That's when it got more serious.

Everyone pretty much says they are nervous for their first Iditarod. It's a big event and they're going out there for the first time. But I'd like to think that I was pretty calm and cool. There was definitely some nerves and stress, but I had been to the start before. I had been there and seen what it was like, the excitement and the level of craziness. I had put a lot of miles on my team in training and I felt I was ready to do it.

For my rookie year I was driving a team that had raced hard that year and the year before. It was exciting, but within reason. As I said, I had been to the start before. I probably took it all for granted. I grew up with dogs and it was cool to be part of the Iditarod. That's generally how I felt. It was a relief when we left the starting line and the race was actually underway. It was a relief to be going.

Usually, a musher has spent a long time thinking of getting into the Iditarod so for the first race, when it actually starts and you head out onto the trail, it's one of the most rewarding feelings. That's how I think about it. It's hard to explain.

The Iditarod is one thousand miles long and the weather changes and you don't get much sleep and you have to take care of the dogs. It's emotional because it's so full of ups and downs. There are plenty of times that you feel you can't go any farther. Sleep deprivation has a lot to do with your mood. When you're sleep deprived you see things that are not necessarily the way they are. It's hard to be a good judge of how your dog team is doing when you are sleep deprived.

In the area of Ophir and Cripple it was fifty below zero according to the thermometer on my sled. That was the only time I felt discouraged. It probably actually got to fifty-five or sixty below. That was a cold race. That was probably my hardest race dealing with sleep deprivation and the hardest part of the trail was from Nikolai to McGrath. I would fall asleep while I was running. It sounds impossible, but, well, it's possible.

When you get to Nome, and you go under the burled arch, it feels great. You've gotten through those tough moments and it's all worth it in the end.

We have a small kennel of about twenty-five dogs. Living off the road system in Alaska is hard. Everything is more expensive and travel is harder. That's the norm. I've gotten used to it so far. It can turn into a terribly expensive thing, though. If I buy a bale of straw in Anchorage it costs $13, but then I have to ship it to Bethel. By the time it gets here to me the cost is $35 for that bale. It's just ridiculously expensive. It's hard to be a dog musher out here in the Bush. I have thought about moving onto the road system, but I don't know if I'm ready to do that.

The more Iditarods you do the more you realize that they are all different. For sure I have learned more since I started. Sometimes learning more, you don't know if that's better or worse. I just glanced at my trophies from the Iditarod the other day and I notice that my times have gotten slower. My fifth-place finish was slower than my eighth-place finish. I was thinking, *Uh, what the heck is going on here?*

You should learn each time you do the Iditarod and that you train for the Iditarod. You spend hundreds and hundreds of hours in one place on the runners in the back of a sled. All you can do is think.

Things changed for me in a hurry in the Iditarod. In my first one in 2009 all I wanted to do is finish. Then, when I finished eighth in my second race in 2011, my thinking changed. At the start all I was thinking about was to just finish as high as I could. But it all came together so well in the race. Things worked out perfectly and I snuck into the top ten right at the end of the race. At the finish I went, "Damn, top ten, sweet."

And then I finished fifth. I had just gotten started. So now the goal is to win the Iditarod. I don't know how many years it will take, but the goal is to win. Once I finished eighth and it was only my second Iditarod I thought right away, *This is possible.*

Jim LANIER

A retired doctor in Chugiak, Jim Lanier, seventy-four, knows what it takes to stay young—mush the one thousand miles of the Iditarod Trail. Born in Washington, D.C., Lanier grew up in North Dakota and moved to Alaska in 1967. He spent more than thirty years working for Providence Hospital in Anchorage.

Lanier developed an interest in mushing in 1977 and he entered his first Iditarod in 1979. Lanier has participated in seventeen Iditarods spread out over thirty-five years, but most heavily in the 2000s and virtually with no gaps in recent years. Well-conditioned and trim, Lanier looks much younger than his age, and acts it on the trail, too. Lanier has four children [three grown] and five grandchildren.

His best finish was eighteenth in 2004 and he finished twentieth in 2008. Married to Anna Bondarenko, the first Russian woman to race in the Iditarod in 2000, Lanier is also author of the recently released Iditarod memoir *Beyond Ophir.* At the time of this interview Bondarenko was translating Lanier's book into Russian with the hopes portions would appear in the Russian *Reader's Digest.*

As one of his mushing distinctions Lanier has competed in and completed at least one Iditarod in every decade since the 1970s, or in every decade the Iditarod has been in existence. In 2003, Lanier won the Iditarod Sportsmanship Award.

What got me started in the Iditarod in the first place was the appeal of the dogs. Actually, another thing that got me started was that on January 1, 1974, when I returned to Alaska after doing my pathology residency at the Mayo Clinic, there was a photograph on the front page of the *Anchorage Times* of a woman I knew named Judy Gould and she was driving a dog team in a sprint race.

Her hair was flying and she had a wild look on her face and I thought, *That looks terrific.* Up until that point I had only been a mushing spectator. At that moment I thought, *Why not me?* It looked like so much wild, crazy fun. So then her husband, Ron, took over the kennel and he started talking to me about mushing. We got into a lead-dog contest, which I won, the only time I ever won anything. This lead-dog contest was on a slalom-like course on Fourth Avenue in Anchorage during the Fur Rendezvous. They don't have it anymore.

Things kind of went from there. I got my kids a husky puppy, a Siberian husky, which is the only Siberian I ever owned, and started the Siberian pulling me on a bicycle the next summer. Then I got a few more dogs and a sled and everything went downhill from there. One dog at a time. It's hard to stop once you start to accumulate dogs or wives or whatever. I have about fifty dogs. No plans to stop doing the Iditarod yet.

Mushing did live up to my image of it after seeing that picture in the newspaper. It did. I still really enjoy zipping down a trail. I think it's taken on a whole different dimension than just being out mushing with the dogs. It's been put in a whole other gear. Of course the race has changed since the 1970s.

In 1979, when I first entered the Iditarod, I was totally inexperienced. I had never done any race before, not even a three-mile sprint. That race was my most memorable of all. It was such an eye-opener and a learning experience. It was much tougher than races I've done since then. And I was a lot younger then, but still, it was so tough. The trail was really tougher than it is now. It wasn't as well-established and not nearly as well marked. When conditions got tough at night with a whiteout or whatnot, at times it was virtually impossible to stay on the trail. You just bushwhacked all over the place. A five-hour run would take you ten hours, if you made it at all that night. So it was harder in all ways.

I had never raced before and jumped into a one-thousand-mile race. Of course, you can't do that now because everyone is required to qualify by completing other, shorter races. But that's the way it was then. I don't know if I thought it was the greatest thing I've ever done, but it was the craziest thing I've ever done. I was really glad to have done it and I enjoy reliving the moments and telling people about it. I took a lot of nice photographs that first race. I finished forty-third and it took me over twenty-four days. A couple of years ago I did the Iditarod in ten days and five hours.

My first thought when I finished was, *Where's the beer?* After that I was looking for a little sleep. Then when you get a little bit of rest you realize how much fun it is in Nome right after the race. After the beer comes a snooze, which is five or six hours instead of the twelve you might expect. Then you start to appreciate Nome itself. I think that's your first take on the return to normal life. That's a big reason for getting to Nome—how much fun it is there for the few days you spend after the race—all the activities, all of the friends that you make over the years.

Then when you go home, you start to dream about next time. It doesn't take long. It's pretty much right away. I never thought, *I'm never doing this again.* I did not predict that I would still be doing the Iditarod thirty-five years later. In fact, after 1979 I didn't do another dog race for five years. And after that it was another fourteen years before I did another Iditarod. At the time I was thinking, *Maybe I'll do one and maybe I won't.* But since 1998 I've done one just about every year. There were two gaps. In 2000 I sat out and I helped Anna. And then in 2011 I had hip replacement surgery and I had to sit that one out. Now it's, "Of course I'm going to do the Iditarod."

I was a pathologist, microscope work and a laboratory. I've been retired six years now and that has been great, giving me time for other things. I'm not sure how I pulled off training for the Iditarod when I was working full-time. There's more time for mushing, but there's more time for everything.

The biggest attraction for me now is just being out on the trail, whether it's doing the Iditarod or other races, or just being out running and training. Another big part of it all is everything else that comes with mushing and the race, the friends you make, the mushers, volunteers, and people you meet.

That all sticks with you. The great places you visit like the villages and the identity of being an Iditarod musher is a great thing to have.

I have to admit that when people ask me what I do and I say, "I run dogs" they ask, "Have you ever done the Iditarod?" I can say, "Oh yes, several times." They go, "Really?" Then you get into talking about it. It's a somewhat repeated conversation, but it's always fun.

There are so many parts of the Iditarod I enjoy, the music, the singing of the national anthem and the Alaska Flag Song at the banquet, and then the singing at the church in Nome at the finish line where they have a special service on Sunday morning. I look forward to that as much as the finishers' banquet. We tell tales and I've gotten into composing a song for the banquet and I sing a song every year. It was years before I did a song.

While the 1979 race was my most memorable, there have been a lot of times when things have caught me by surprise on the trail. The first race was so tough because I was green and the weather was tough, cold and windy. In 1984, it was a swimming race. It rained on the first part of the race and we had deep water. That was a grind. There was a race a few years ago where we had what I call an Arctic hurricane. Iditarod insider folks called it "Dancing with Wind" or something like that. For two solid days the wind was really fierce.

I was on the Yukon River out of Grayling and Eagle Island. It just about did me in. There have been a lot of times like that. I've been out in colder than minus fifty, but a couple of years ago I was on the way to Unalakleet out of Kaltag. It had been a cold race, minus thirty and worse, and I had about thirty miles to Unalakleet when the sun came up. Just when the sun comes up it tends to get a little colder for a little while. Something about the sun's rays hitting paradoxically makes it colder and it was already minus forty. I was already really cold. I had everything I could on, warmers, my mitts, and boots, and then it dropped down into a low spot as the sun first cracked and it got really cold. It was just as the heaters in my mitts went out. I hadn't replenished them. I had had frostbite a long time ago—it started in my first race—and my fingers are super sensitive. My thermometer read minus forty-nine.

All of a sudden I realized my hands were freezing and I realized they were working so poorly that I wouldn't be able to replenish the heaters. I wanted to break out new heaters, but if I tried my hands would get colder still. So I just went on. If the dogs had gotten tangled I don't think I would have been able to untangle them. I ran for another twenty-five or thirty miles. We just kept motoring. Nothing untoward happened. By the time we got there the sun was higher in the sky and things were warming up and I was OK.

Every year during the race there are one or two times where something like that happens and I wonder if I'm going to make it: *Will I finish the race? Am I going to make it to the next checkpoint?* It might be something because of me, the dogs, or the equipment. You repress a lot, but you also hope maybe next year will be different and nothing will happen.

My favorite race was the first one, but the one in 2004 that I did with Anna was really fun. We trained together, which isn't always good because we have such different styles of training, so after that we trained separately. We went into the race separately and somebody asked me, "What's your goal this year?" I said, "To beat my wife." That was Anna's second Iditarod. [Lanier had his best finish that year, but Anna scratched.]

I refer to the Iditarod as "The Last Great Race on Earth" and I love talking about it with Iditarod people and even people who don't know anything about it. I enjoy it all. Not as many people know about it Outside, even if it is getting more significantly better known, but you can still run into people who say, "Idita-What?" There are some people left who still don't know the word. People are fascinated by it, though. Just about the first thing people say when you talk about it is, "Well, I could never do it." Which is probably true. Anyone who thinks that way would probably not want to do it. I think the cold would be too much for them. The cold is what people say would bother them.

The Iditarod is a wildly popular event. People love to follow it in the media and out on the trail. Being part of the event is one reason I do it. My family has been very supportive. My wife, Anna, has done the race. My daughter Kim did the Junior Iditarod. When my son Jimmy turns eighteen in 2015—I'll be seventy-five then—maybe we'll have three teams in the race at once.

CHAPTER 28

Aliy ZIRKLE

I t has been apparent for the last few years that Aliy Zirkle and husband, Allen Moore, have one of the top dog yards going in their SP Kennel. In both 2012 and 2013 Zirkle finished second in the Iditarod and in both 2013 and 2014 Moore won the Yukon Quest. Then in 2014 Zirkle seemed to have the race title within her grasp, only to be forced by vicious winds to take shelter in Safety, just twenty-two miles from the finish line. She was passed by Dallas Seavey in an epic race, falling short of victory by two minutes twenty-two seconds, but finishing in a time below the old record. It was a race where the trail and weather were so rough at different points that about twenty mushers scratched.

Overall, Zirkle and Moore, a Two Rivers, Alaska, couple, have pretty much been the hottest mushers in the world with their top-notch results in the one-thousand-mile races. Zirkle, forty-five, won the 2000 Yukon Quest and then began her Iditarod mushing career. Long considered a top racer whom other contenders kept their eye on, she has made her biggest breakthrough over the last couple of years. Zirkle had eight top-twenty finishes in her first thirteen Iditarods since 2001. Zirkle has twice won the Humanitarian Award.

Originally from New Hampshire, Zirkle graduated from the University of Pennsylvania with a degree in biology and moved to Alaska in 1990 where she worked for the US Fish and Wildlife Service. Zirkle is a full-time musher who gives talks to tourists in the summer. Blessed with a one-thousand-watt smile, long blonde hair, and striking looks, Zirkle has always been a photogenic musher.

Zirkle's main goal is to win the Iditarod title with a team of fresh-looking dogs and take home one of the prized pickup trucks the winner receives. She would love to be the third woman to win the Iditarod after Libby Riddles and Susan Butcher, and the first since 1990.

The 2013 race from the start figured to be interesting because it was not predictable. There was incredibly strange weather. You think you're going to be mushing in cold weather in the wintertime and it turns out to be spring. You're hoping it isn't breakup. The mushers' strategies were all over the board and the weather was all over the board.

You had to really focus on yourself. You couldn't get wrapped up in what others were doing. What matters are your team and your race. Especially early in the race I don't get all worked up by what other people are doing because I adamantly believe that however my race turns out is how my dogs can do and how my team can do. So for me it's pretty irrelevant how everyone else's team can do. It's up to our squad. I came into the race having finished second the year before so I thought it might be my turn to win.

I try to break up the Iditarod into thirds. The first third of every Iditarod is really trying to figure out where you're going to set the bar for your team. You have to stay towards the front, but you don't necessarily have to be in front. You have to keep your team healthy and you have to stay healthy.

After the first third of the race I was pretty happy with my squad. Of course you compare your time to everyone, but you've also got to look at your team. The first third is not very far. You can make up a lot of time and distance during the running of the race. The second three hundred miles is where you really kind of have to have confidence in your squad and its stamina. You can either stay near the top or go to the top. It's one of those two things.

My strategy is different than most people's. What I do at checkpoints might be different than what most people are doing, but that's what I'm comfortable doing and my dogs are comfortable doing. You don't know what other people are doing. Sometimes that's better for me. In the second third of the race I thought I made some mistakes out there, but it turns out they weren't mistakes at all.

That left the last third of the race. That's when I learned that my second third was successful because I had this rocket ship to navigate to the finish line. That made me very happy. The dogs were strong, enthusiastic, and ready to go. I asked them to do as much as I could have being fair and square, and Mitch Seavey beat me by twenty-three minutes.

It was really close. I always thought it was possible that I was going to win, but I don't ever let myself think, *Hey, what color truck am I gonna have?* No, never for a moment. That's way too much pressure to put on your team. I don't even think Mitch probably thought he was going to win until five miles from the finish line. I'm not putting words in his mouth, but I think it's hard to say you have it in the can in a dog race unless you're twelve hours in front of everyone.

I left Koyuk in fifth place and I came up over the horizon and saw two teams parked camping and went right by them. I thought, *Well, that just bumped me up a whole bunch.* So you never really knew what to expect and it made it pretty creative.

It got pretty close at night and I was coming down from the Topkok Hills and Mitch was parked on the lagoon down there feedings dogs a meal. I was not that far from him distance-wise, but by the time I got to the bottom of the hill he was two-thirds of a mile ahead of me. Mitch's team was always faster than mine on the flats. I thought I needed to catch him on the hills and thought I got pretty close to him. I didn't catch him.

At Safety [twenty-two miles from Nome] I was still in it, I thought. I could still see him [Seavey]. He was still right there and he hadn't won yet, so there's always a chance. He hadn't gotten there. Going around Cape Nome is always a fun adventure and I put a whole bunch into getting over it as fast as I could, running and scooting up there. I didn't see him anymore. It was sunset right when I went around the corner of Cape Nome and I'm sure he wasn't going to look back with a headlight. You don't turn around and look with your headlight.

So coming down Cape Nome you can't tell where you are because you see a lot of lights in Nome and on the outskirts. I couldn't really tell where he was. I was being pretty enthusiastic trying to catch him, though. There is a road crossing where there were a whole bunch of people, after the Nome River, and I yelled, "Where is he?" Somebody said he just crossed the finish line. It was probably three miles out or something like that. I hadn't thought of who was behind me or anything. Perhaps then I started looking back and wondering how far anyone was behind me, but until then it hadn't really crossed my mind.

A lot of times if a race is that close there is second-guessing, but not in this race. If I made any errors, everybody made them. It was not a straight-forward Iditarod, so it was a free-for-all where a lot of weird stuff happened. We were swimming through open water. My run into Nome from White Mountain wasn't a smooth run, but there's nothing I could have done at a particular moment that would have improved it.

So I finished in second place for the second year in a row. I feel good and bad about that. I'm proud of my dogs and I always felt like I could win, so it doesn't surprise me that I did so well. But second place is hard to digest for me. It's great that our dogs are proving to be this phenomenal, upbeat. We don't have three hundred dogs and we don't buy and sell dogs. They're our dogs, the same dogs that they've always been, the grandkids of the grandparent dogs that I've had. I'd rather come in forty-ninth with my dogs than first with someone else's dogs, so they made me very proud. I'd like to see them come in ahead of anyone else, that's for sure, but it hasn't happened yet.

It was always possible, but I guess this makes it seem more possible. I always thought I could win, but this adds confidence in me to everyone else. Everyone is like, "Wow, Aliy came in second place." But I'm going, "Yeah, but I didn't come in first."

It's a phenomenal group of dogs. Allen won the Quest and eleven of the Yukon Quest dogs were on my Iditarod team. They were second, and I like first better. Yeah, I'm proud, but no, I'm not satisfied. It's amazing to me how many years and Iditarods have gone by since I moved over from the Quest. It doesn't seem like it should have been that long.

I think I am almost more proud of starting and finishing every race than I am of the seconds. I think that shows more of my character, and second place shows character. I've had a tremendous career thus far and it's been dependent on the dogs. If have a team that I can push and win with, I will. If I have a team that I can't, then I'll come in twenty-fifth or something like that. If you're not winning, whatever it is, the place is slightly irrelevant. If I'm first it's great, but if I'm tenth I might as well be twenty-fourth or thirtieth. Not everyone would say that.

Higher places in the Iditarod pay more money, but money in the Iditarod is irrelevant. I won $48,000 for second place and that's not something to scoff at, but it's irrelevant. Aaron Burmeister was running right up there and he came in eleventh, so you can win $48,000 or in the blink of an eye you can get $11,000. So I never count on race money for anything. Ever. It's like a bonus. If I make some money, that's great. I don't, I don't ever think I'm going to make money. It's nothing I counted on. I mean I stopped in Safety one year and lost five or six places because I didn't feel like pushing the dogs. I had a cup of coffee and some Cheetos, and came in twenty-ninth. But twenty-fifth to thirty-fifth places, it's like la-di-da. If you're not winning, it doesn't necessarily matter to me.

I know everything about my team that I need to know. It's everyone else that might look at it and think something, but I'm not racing for everyone else. I'm racing to win and after that whatever I come in I know how my dogs fared. I'm a lot smarter about the race than I used to be. I'm always learning, but when I started running the Iditarod I didn't assume I knew much about racing. I never thought I knew anything when I started dog racing because I didn't get into dogs to race. I just had dogs for fun because I like dogs. I've learned a lot about theory and strategy certainly, but it all comes back to having a phenomenal group of dogs that are dedicated to you and that you trained appropriately and that are ready to race. I think it all comes down to that and a little bit of good fortune.

Over time I've evolved my training strategy to what I think is better. You know everyone over time hopefully improves to what they think is better. Whether it truly is better or not, I don't know. Right now Allen and I are in mushing long-term. I don't think fifty is old. I haven't thought fifty is old for a long time. I don't know how long is the right time. We're pretty happy in our lives. We certainly have a schedule and a plan for our lives. We make a pretty good living doing what we do.

In the summer I greet passengers on the Alaska Railroad when they stop and talk to them about mushing. We work a lot. We [Moore and Zirkle] actually should probably take more time off. I would say we enjoy dog mushing because of the dogs, the adventure, and the outdoors, and because it keeps us really fit. We like being fit and healthy. If we were to stop doing the life that we live now everything would be different. Anything we chose would be very different, so I don't even know what direction that we would go in.

I'll always have dogs, but we have a comfortable life, and if we were to stop racing I bet we'd come up with something else interesting.

About the
AUTHOR

*L*ew Freedman is a veteran newspaper sportswriter and experienced author of more than seventy books. He spent seventeen years at the *Anchorage Daily News* in Alaska and wrote extensively about the Iditarod Trail Sled Dog Race. He has written several books about the Iditarod and had stories appear in *Alaska Magazine* and *Alaska Airlines* magazine.

Freedman has also worked for the *Chicago Tribune* and *Philadelphia Inquirer*. A frequent traveler to Alaska, Freedman believes the Iditarod is one of the world's great sporting events and only wishes the dogs could talk so he could better write their story.

He and his wife, Debra, live in Indiana.